Brasted

the past in pictures

Roger Rogowski

BRASTED
SOCIETY

Published by The Brasted Society

Contents

Acknowledgements 4

Introduction 5

A brief history of photography and the picture postcard 9

Chapter 1 – The Village Green 11

Chapter 2 – The High Street 24

Chapter 3 – St Martin's Church and Church Road 40

Chapter 4 - Rectory Lane and Brasted Hill Road 52

Chapter 5 – Brasted Chart and Toys Hill 58

Chapter 6 – The Big Houses 68

Chapter 7 – The Railway 77

Chapter 8 – Village Life 84

Chapter 9 – Brasted Miscellany 101

Further reading 116

Image Credits 118

Index 120

Acknowledgements

The idea for this book came from Rob Peake who was born and raised in Brasted and who has accumulated a large collection of picture postcards of Brasted. As Karina Jackson and I have both separately accumulated similar collections of old photographs, Rob suggested collating them into a book. Karina, as the archivist for Brasted, has also received donations of many artefacts, including old photographs.

As the project developed, it soon became apparent that there were other significant local collections of old photographs of Brasted that needed to be included. I am therefore grateful to all who kindly contributed pictures and postcards to the project including Brasted Church, Brasted Eleemosynary Charities, Brasted Village Hall Trust, Marc Draper, Frank George, Pam Day, Lorna Grosse, Bob Ogley, Elizabeth Rich and Bill Curtis of the Westerham Society. I am also grateful to Keith and Celia Smith for the use of some photographs displayed in the Millennium Exhibition that they organised in 2000, at the same time creating the Brasted Archive, which is now managed by Karina. A full list of acknowledgements for the photographs and other images used appears under 'Image Credits' at the back of this book.

As well as sharing their photographs, thanks are again due to Karina Jackson and Rob Peake for their advice on some of the historical detail in the captions; Karina again for creating digital copies of many of the photographs from Keith and Celia Smith's local history exhibition in 2000; to Terry Hope for his professional advice on my summary of the history of photography and to my wife Chrissie for proofreading the final draft. Last, but not least, thanks must go to Bill Chopping for the huge amount of work he put in laying out the book, improving the quality of many of the images, presenting countless alternative suggestions for almost every aspect of the book and generally seeing it into publication.

Roger Rogowski

Introduction

Brasted is in the Vale of Holmesdale, about four miles to the west of Sevenoaks and two miles east of Westerham in north west Kent. Brasted is approximately one mile wide east to west and five miles wide north to south and borders the parish of Sundridge with Ide Hill to the east and Westerham to the west.

Brasted is both a civil and ecclesiastical parish in the Sevenoaks district of Kent and includes the smaller settlements of Brasted Chart and Toys Hill although Toys Hill is in the ecclesiastical parish of Sundridge with Ide Hill. The population of Brasted has changed little in the last 150 years, having a population of 1,429 in the 2011 census and 1,182 in the 1861 census, about the time the earliest photographs of Brasted were taken.

The place name originates from the old Saxon words *brade*, meaning length, and *stede*, a place. Brasted was recorded as Briestede in the Domesday Book (1086) and Bradstede in the Textus Roffensis (1122-1124) although there is archaeological evidence of a Saxon church on the site of St Martin's Church.

Until the sixteenth century, the village was almost certainly situated around the church or between the church and the Pilgrims Way, which was the main east – west route through the area before the marshland around the River Darent was drained during the sixteenth century. In addition to being the main thoroughfare through the village, the Pilgrims Way as its name suggests had long served as a route for pilgrims travelling to the shrine of Thomas à Becket at Canterbury. Although there is archaeological evidence that the route dates back to at least 600-450 BC, it is thought that it was probably in existence in the Stone Age. After the valley was drained, the east – west road through the valley, now designated as the A25, evolved to become the main road and the centre of the village developed as we know it today.

Agricultural and local trades predominated for many centuries and, up to the late nineteenth and early twentieth centuries, Brasted was a largely rural community with a mix of farms and large estates dominating the district. In common with other relatively small communities, Brasted was fairly self-sufficient in providing almost everything that people might need for everyday living, such as shops, schools and the like and also for their work. The need to provide these facilities also gave work and business opportunities to local people. London, although only some 20 miles to the north, was a world away.

In the early twentieth century, car ownership and, before that, the ownership of horse powered transportation, was far from commonplace. Travel to nearby towns like Sevenoaks and Westerham was an exception rather than the rule. The coming of the Westerham to Dunton Green railway in 1881, was relatively late in the evolution of railways and, although it was originally planned that the railway would be extended to Oxted in the west, it was never completed adding, to a degree, to Brasted's relative isolation.

Four of the oldest images of Brasted in this book are from the very early days of photography. A photograph of St Martin's Church taken in 1857, is probably the oldest existing photograph of Brasted, recording the building as it looked before alterations were carried out in 1866 when the roof and North and South walls of the nave were demolished in preparation for expansion on both sides of the church. A photograph of the White Hart is dated 1866, before it was rebuilt in 1885, and a photograph of the Old Rectory, which was the rector's residence at the time, is dated 1869. The children in the photograph of the Old Rectory are almost certainly posed and the slight blurring of the background to the left is a function of a relatively short depth of field, a by-product of using a slow exposure speed as photographic film technology was still in its infancy. Finally, an undated photograph, thought to be from about 1865, of what was known as Ford's Cottages opposite the White Hart is at a casual glance very similar to the same scene today but, on further study, reveals some significant differences.

At first glance, many of the photographs in the book feature scenes that look almost exactly the same as they do today. However, look more closely and the details in many of the photographs reveal evidence of that different way of life: the diversity of the shops and businesses, how much of everyday life was played out in the streets and fields and as a close knit community, the sometimes startlingly evident gap between rich and poor, and of course, an almost complete absence of road traffic indicating how little movement there was between villages. Change is an ongoing process and as if to emphasise the steady decline of local industry and general employment and the sense of community, while compiling this book, R. Durtnell and Sons, Britain's oldest builder having been founded in 1591 and who built many properties in the local area, ceased trading in 2019. The future of the Fox and Hounds and Stanhope Arms, after being in the balance for most of 2020, has been settled. Sadly, the Fox and Hounds has been lost but the Stanhope has been saved.

Many more postcards were produced than are contained in this book. There were evidently favourite or more 'commercial' views of Brasted, which were reproduced time and again such as the village green, St Martin's Church and the White Hart, while other views of Brasted only ever appeared on one or two postcards. Rather than include multiple versions of those more commercial views, which often differed only by being taken from a slightly different angle, this book only contains a selection of those scenes, and this has been done primarily to show how the same scene evolved over time.

Photography was still obviously in its infancy at the time that many of these photographs were taken and, of course, some of the images have faded over time. The quality of some of the images is unfortunately less than ideal and, where they are, they have been selected anyway if their content warrants inclusion regardless of quality, although many have been restored for this book to remove age related blemishes and to improve the clarity of images wherever possible and where doing so significantly improved the image. As an example, the 1857 photograph of St Martin's Church has been heavily restored for this book. The original was badly damaged when a V1 flying bomb exploded to the east of the church in July 1944 and some assumptions have been made about the detail in the parts of the original photograph that are missing.

Many of the old postcards reproduced in this book are clearly over-marked either 'M. Davis' or 'The Stores – W Withers and Sons'. The owners of these two longstanding shops that used to operate in the High Street, long since closed, were evidently enterprising enough to recognise the commercial potential of picture postcards to produce their own for sale. Look carefully at M. Davis' postcards and you will see the same small boy, who was apparently his son, appearing in the foreground each time, now a small piece of personal history in each photograph.

In deciding how to present the large collection of images in this book, they fell naturally into two distinct categories. Where they could be placed in distinct geographic areas, these appear in the first five chapters. The large number of interesting images of the High Street available necessitated splitting them into two separate chapters - for the village green, together with the White Hart, and the rest of the High Street. As far as possible, the images in these first five chapters are ordered by geographical location rather than chronological sequence, so that the reader can follow a trail around each part of the parish, either physically by walking with the book or mentally. Anyone familiar with the parish boundary will spot that a large part of the parish, about a quarter of which lies to the north of the M25, is not represented in this book for the simple reason that we were unable to find any old photographs or postcards of this area. The appeal of this part of Brasted lies mostly in nature as it includes part of the North Downs and the Pilgrims Way and, perhaps if we had found any, those scenes would probably appear very similar to how they look today.

The final four chapters are thematic for a number of reasons, primarily because they feature photographs that are not linked to any specific part of Brasted. The very large and interesting houses that are or were scattered fairly evenly across the parish deserve a chapter of their own both for their architectural interest and their interesting stories. The most prominent of these is Brasted Place, which was the home of the lords of the manor for hundreds of years and was later occupied by prominent figures including Dr John Turton, physician to King George III; Prince Louis-Napoléon Bonaparte, who later became Emperor Napoléon III of France; and William Tipping, industrialist, politician and a great benefactor to Brasted who funded many improvements to the village in his lifetime. Similarly, the railway, which ran between Dunton Green and its terminus in Westerham for eighty years from 1881, bisected the parish east to west roughly where the M25 now runs.

The photographs in the penultimate chapter, in contrast to those in the preceding chapters, which look at places, are more focused on local people whether at work, rest or play. All except one of the images in this chapter are photographs from private collections and not postcards emphasising the role of the picture postcard as a medium for sharing scenic views more than people and activities. In the course of looking for images for this book, a number of items of local ephemera from the nineteenth and early twentieth centuries also came to light, many of which relate to places, events and businesses featured in some of the photographs, many of which supplement the photographs in the preceding chapters and they seemed too good not to include. These have been given their own chapter at the end of the book.

Many of the photographs and postcards appearing in this book are dated and these are as dated or postmarked on the original which, in the case of postcards, is of course not necessarily when the photograph was taken. In some cases, where multiple copies of the same postcard were available, the earliest postmark has been used to get as close as possible to the original date of the image. Where photographs or postcards are undated, the date has been estimated based on evidence in the image and these are indicated by 'about' in front of the date. To quote one example, the latest dated postcard of the High Street without telegraph poles that we have found is 1907 while the oldest card featuring telegraph poles, which were installed on the south side of the road only, is dated 1912 and the presence or absence of telegraph poles has been used in dating some postcards of the High Street.

If there seems to be a sense of nostalgia for old and better times in this introduction, it should also be said that times were very harsh for the majority of people living in Brasted up until the late nineteenth and early twentieth century, who lived and worked in conditions that we can hardly imagine today. More than a hundred people in the parish, about 10% of the population at the time, received essential poor relief, often in the form of gifts such as sacks of coal, boots or lengths of cloth from which to make clothes. Today, Brasted is a great place to live. Close to all of the modern essentials available in nearby towns and with excellent transport links to London, other parts of the country and beyond with the Channel Tunnel terminus and at least two international airports under an hour's drive away. At the same time, Brasted is a friendly and welcoming community for those who wish to be a part of it and we are surrounded by beautiful countryside in a Designated Area of Outstanding Natural Beauty, much of it managed by the National Trust.

It has been a fascinating project collating this collection of photographs and other images from various sources and compiling the accompanying captions in which I have attempted to provide additional historical information rather than just describing what we can all see in the images. I hope the photographs and captions provide an interesting and new insight into your knowledge of Brasted and this beautiful part of Kent and that you enjoy your tour of Brasted as it was many years ago!

Roger Rogowski

A brief history of photography and the picture postcard

The taking of photographs by a chemical process is receding into history as a result of the introduction of digital photography in the late twentieth century with so-called wet film photography now generally only used by professional photographers and hobbyists. Developments in photography started about two hundred years ago as various early experiments were conducted to produce a lasting photographic image without success until Joseph Nicéphore Niépce, a French inventor, produced the first durable, light-fast camera photograph in around 1824.

About a decade later, Louis Daguerre introduced his daguerreotype process, which produced detailed permanent photographs on silver-plated copper plates while William Henry Fox Talbot started to produce more durable camera negatives on paper. Wet film photographs are produced in 'negative' because the lightest areas of the subject act more quickly on the light-sensitive chemicals on the photographic film, while the dark areas of the subject act on the chemicals more slowly. This image is then reversed in a 'darkroom' on paper or card, a darkroom being required to prevent extraneous light acting on the light sensitive chemicals before the image is 'fixed' with further chemicals.

The problem with early photography was that exposure times – the time required to create a photographic image – were impractically long and it wasn't until this improved in the early 1840s that photography started to become a commercial proposition in the following decade. Even then, exposure times were long by the standards that most people will remember in the second half of the twentieth century before digital photography, to the extent that photographing moving subjects was impossible. Anyone familiar with informal photographs of people taken outdoors from the mid-nineteenth and even in the very early twentieth century will have seen that some people appear to be blurred or even appear to be in two places at once in the same image as the slow exposure speeds of the time meant that everyone had to stand or sit still for long periods in order to produce a sharp image. This also explains why even crowds of people in very old photographs are often obviously posed, sometimes leaning against or holding a fixed object to ensure they remain as still as possible. Long film exposures also partly explain why people in early photographs often carried serious expressions although, in the period when portrait photography was still very much in competition with portrait paintings, the generally accepted convention of smiling for the camera was still some way in the future. Anyone who has tried to hold a smile while having their photograph taken by someone constantly fiddling with their camera will know how difficult it is.

From the beginning of photography, images were monochromatic, more commonly known as black and white, as experiments in achieving satisfactory colour photographs were largely unsuccessful both in terms of quality and commercial viability. Although there are striking colour images dating from Victorian times, these relied on expensive and painstaking processes and it was only much later, in the 1930s, when Agfa and Kodak introduced commercially viable colour film, which fairly accurately reproduced the colours of the subject. Before then, sepia, a brown pigment derived from the ink of cuttlefish, was used to mitigate against fading as early photographs were prone to do. At the same time, the shades of brown produced by sepia created a 'warmer' look when compared with shades of grey in monochromatic photographs. Often, old black and white photographs are referred to as appearing to be faded although, after many years, sepia photographs also often appear faded.

9

To create multi-coloured photographs in the days before the widespread availability of colour film, black and white images were sometimes hand tinted, an obviously labour intensive process. These photographs from that period often look almost like paintings, which in some respects, they are. For aesthetic reasons, any sepia photographs used in this book have been converted back to their original black and white appearance but the few hand tinted photographs in the book are reproduced in their original colours. The difference between hand tinted and original black and white photographs is well demonstrated by comparing the photograph on the front cover with the same image in the 'High Street' chapter. The image on the front cover has been taken from a hand tinted postcard, which has an interesting quality. The sky, roofs and trees have been hand tinted but the walls, pavement, road and boys have been left in the original black and white form.

Almost all of us who remember a time before digital photography probably tend to forget, and certainly anyone under the age of about thirty will never really appreciate, how precious photographic film was. 35mm film, the most popular type of photographic film before the introduction of digital photography, was generally supplied on a reel of 24 or 36 exposures. I was given my first camera, a Kodak Brownie 44A, when I was ten years old and a standard reel of film for that camera contained only 12 exposures. That meant that everyone, from ten year old boys to professional photographers, was relatively selective about the photographs they took.

When photography was in its infancy in the nineteenth century, photographs were taken on a single plate which was both costly to purchase and very heavy particularly when compared to film. The scale of change in our attitude to and use of photography is probably best emphasised by the estimate that more photographs are now taken every two minutes worldwide than were taken in the whole of the nineteenth century.

An estimated 380 billion photographs are now taken every year. Even when photography became affordable by the general public in the 1930s and towards the end of the period covered by this book, photographers were only snapping away at a rate of about a billion photographs per year.

Mobile communication is generally taken for granted today although the introduction of telephones as a common feature in people's homes is still just about within living memory, so the idea that the only way to communicate with someone long distance would be to write to them seems alien to almost everyone now. The use of blank postcards as a means of sending messages dates back almost to the introduction of the postage stamp in 1840 but it required the permission of the Royal Mail to allow the posting of picture postcards in the UK in 1894. To enable reasonably rapid - for the time – communications, the post was often collected and delivered multiple times per day even in relatively rural locations like Brasted.

Almost overnight, the sending of picture postcards became hugely popular and the demand led to the production of picture postcards of almost every subject. The tradition of sending picture postcards is now in severe decline as we are able to send personal photos instantly to friends via social media platforms like Instagram and Facebook but the so-called 'golden age' of picture postcards, in the first half of the twentieth century, has left us with a fantastic legacy. For us today, it is a means by which we can see good quality images of almost every road, major building or landmark in the country as it looked around a hundred years ago. Brasted is no exception and the often referred to 'golden age' of picture postcards, together with early photographs, allows us to see what the village and the surrounding settlements were like in the late nineteenth and early twentieth centuries when rural life was very different.

Chapter 1

The Village Green

Although lying towards the eastern end of Brasted, the village green has been the focal point of the village for many years, at one time featuring a lock-up, a small jail for securing local villains pending trial or as a punishment for minor offences.

In the past, two of the great estates of Brasted and neighbouring Sundridge respectively, Brasted Place and Combe Bank came almost to the edge of the green, with the entrance road to the former next door to the White Hart and with Combe Bank Lodge, the former entrance to the Combe Bank estate, a few yards to the east of the green.

The village pump on the green is made of cast iron and dates from the nineteenth century and it remained in use until mains water was installed in the surrounding houses. The village sign, representing the Archbishop's Garden, of which Brasted is a part together with neighbouring Sundridge and Westerham, was erected in 1951. An exact replica of the sign, with a new supporting frame and post, was installed in 2017 to replace the original.

During the Second World War, a communal air raid shelter was built on the green as nearby Biggin Hill was a focal point for many aerial battles and, later, many V1 flying bombs fell short of their intended London target creating a random and deadly hazard in the local area. Up until the early twentieth century, Brasted Coachworks and the village wheelwright's workshop were major features of the green situated respectively where the village shop and Old Forge Antiques now stand.

Looking west, 1907, with the White Hart on the left and Ford's Cottages, now called Old White Hart Cottages, on the right. Like much of Brasted, this scene has hardly changed in the intervening years.

Looking west again, 1908, with only the addition of a prominent flagpole distinguishing it from the previous photograph.

The earliest known photograph of the White Hart pub, dated 1866, when the pub was tied to Westerham brewer W Watkins and Son. Note the cottages on the right were demolished to make way for the extension of the White Hart in 1885.

Ford's Cottages, about 1865. The two cottages at the near end of the row were built by John Ford in 1522, while the remaining four cottages were built in 1622 by R Durtnell and Sons, which was Britain's oldest building company, founded in 1591, until their closure in 2019. Note the absence of pavements and the culvert on this side of the road.

Ford's Cottages about 1905, opposite the White Hart. In the intervening years since the photograph on the preceding page, the culvert on the south side of the road has been covered and pavements have been built but horse-drawn transport is still very much in evidence.

The West Kent Foxhounds gather outside the White Hart Hotel. The over-stamp dates this postcard to 1923 when E.J. Keeling took over from G. Sedgwick as proprietor. The gathering of fox hunters was a common sight on Boxing Day in rural communities at one time. The West Kent Foxhounds date back to 1776, founded by John Warde of Squerryes in Westerham, they amalgamated with Old Surrey and Burstow Foxhounds in 1999.

The garden of the White Hart Hotel, 1922, which offered teas on the lawn and tennis for guests. This card shows the telephone number for the White Hart was Brasted 14. These were the days when calls were still connected by telephone operators and the number shows how many telephones there must have been in Brasted at the time!

This postcard of the White Hart is undated but the presence of 'E Preston' on the sign indicates it must date from 1932 onward when Edward and Kathy Preston took over the pub and before 1939 when Croydon brewers Page and Overton acquired it.

The famous black-out board on which fighter pilots based at RAF Biggin Hill signed their names and, on a nearby side panel (not shown) chalked up their latest score of enemy 'kills' during the Second World War. The first signatory was Air Commodore R. (Dicky) Grice in 1942 who was the Commanding Officer at Biggin Hill at the time, the occasion being his leaving party. He was followed by other young men, some of whom quickly became household names as stories of their bravery, daring and decorations became known. The board was later framed as shown on this postcard and was unveiled at the White Hart by Group Captain "Sailor" Malan together with an RAF Ensign, rescued from the RAF Chapel, and presented to the White Hart by the RAF padre, the Reverend Cecil King. The board was later moved to the RAF Museum in Hendon and then to the RAF Club in London and is now on display at the Shoreham Aircraft Museum.

Hand tinted view of the green with the two cottages, still there today, now known as The Hollies and Rosena respectively, about 1910. What is now the village shop just beyond it was a hardware shop at this time.

Looking west, 1941, the addition of the now familiar telephone box, the bus stop and the presence of a car distinguish this scene from how it looked in the previous photograph.

Looking west towards the village green about 1910. Darenton, the imposing house on the other side of the green was built in 1864 as the home of the Durtnell family.

Looking west from the green, about 1905. Horses still provided the main form of transport for short journeys and for transporting light goods, despite the coming of the car, while the new railway between Dunton Green and Westerham, opened in 1881, was being used for longer journeys and to transport heavy goods.

More or less the same view about ten years later. Telegraph poles have been erected on the south side of the High Street in the intervening years. Note the cart on the right-hand side, probably a work in progress for the wheelwright whose shop stood where the antique shop now stands.

Looking east, about 1905. The familiar building on the left, which dates from the sixteenth century, is still a row of four cottages in this photograph. Note the wheelwright's shop, which was demolished in the 1950s.

Looking east again, 1920. The history of the prominent tree on the green is a mystery. Oral accounts tell of an oak tree planted to commemorate the silver jubilee of George V in 1935 although the present tree is a horse chestnut. Traditionally, horse chestnut trees are associated with forge workshops.

An unknown little girl by the village pump, 1926, with the wheelwright's shop in the background. The village pump is cast iron and dates from the nineteenth century and, although it still stands on the green, it was taken out of use when mains water was installed in the surrounding houses.

The village green about 1920, probably taken from the upper storey of what is now the village shop during a meeting of the West Kent Foxhounds. Note the venerable tree, shortly to be replaced by the planting of a new tree to commemorate the silver jubilee of George V in 1935.

Brasted Carriage Works, which stood on the village green where the village shop now stands, about 1870, when the tree in the previous photograph was still young.

This series of photographs from 1900 shows the variety of horse-drawn vehicles produced and repaired by Brasted Carriage works, the quality of their workmanship and the wide geographic area that they served.

A delivery cart for an Otford baker with what looks like a brougham, a two-seater light carriage and the sports coupe of its day, in the background.

Motorised transport replaced horse-drawn vehicles during the early twentieth century although local deliveries were still sometimes made by horse-drawn cart even into the 1950s.

This photograph probably emphasises the range of vehicles produced at the carriage works more than any other, a delivery trap for G White's dairy with a simple hand cart in the background.

Chapter 2
The High Street

The High Street was largely created relatively recently in the sixteenth century when the marshland that characterised the landscape at that time adjacent to the River Darent, was drained. The Pilgrims Way, which runs along the ridge formed by the North Downs about a mile further north, which had been the main east-west through the local area since the Iron Age was largely replaced by what is now known as the A25 in the eighteenth century when a toll road was built from Wrotham Heath to Godstone by the Wrotham Heath Turnpike Trust following an act of Parliament passed in 1765.

Many of the buildings in the High Street date from around the sixteenth to the eighteenth centuries and include many interesting vernacular buildings from the late mediaeval, Queen Anne, Georgian and Victorian periods, respectively to quote some examples, number 17 High Street, Brasted House, Village House and the Village Hall.

Until the 1970s, the High Street was home to a wide variety of shops including a general store selling clothing and furniture; grocery, butcher's, greengrocer's, baker's, newsagent's and chemist's shops. In common with many High Streets, these small businesses were unable to compete with growing car ownership and the rise of the supermarket. By the mid-1980s, only a village store and sub post office, butcher's shop, off licence, newsagent, bank sub-branch, hairdresser's shop and haberdashery remained with other shops being taken over by antique dealers, although even this must seem like a wealth of choice compared to today. In turn, Brasted as a centre for antiques has declined too in recent years although the High Street bears its decline as a retail centre gracefully with many original shopfronts still preserved while the remaining shops bear witness to modern local needs.

The High Street was also home to two pubs, one now offices and one a private house; a village school, now private houses and the village surgery; and a Baptist chapel, also now a private house. The late Victorian village hall in the centre of the High Street, with its ornate Dutch gable and cupola, remains a busy centre for a wide range of activities.

Looking west from the junction with Rectory Lane, about 1905. The posed group of boys and the shopkeeper from Markwick's Stores, the shop on the right, emphasise that the taking of a photograph was an occasion in itself at that time.

Markwick's Stores, about 1910, this is undoubtedly a promotional postcard as they are proudly displaying their delivery van and two delivery bicycles. The shop has changed hands many times but these buildings on the north side of the High Street, close to the junction with Rectory Lane, are still instantly recognisable.

Woodhams store, 1916, further along from Markwick's on the north side of the High Street, occupying what is now Ivy House. Note the shop sign is not in place, which may indicate that O J Woodham has only just taken ownership of the shop.

Woodhams & Sons store, about 1925. Note the delivery bicycle on the right and small boy who may or may not be an intended part of the photograph. Woodhams store sold groceries and also useful household items evidenced by the display on either side of the door in this photograph and the one above.

Looking east with Ford's, later Old White Hart, Cottages clearly visible in the background, about 1915. Those figures are clearly posing for the photograph, something they would be unable to do for very long today. The complete absence of traffic as far as the eye can see clearly demonstrates how life at that time was more locally oriented.

A similar scene some ten years later but traffic is still very light to the extent that the man on the right feels able to walk in the road despite the presence of a wide pavement and the approaching motorcycle.

Looking east, outside Woodhams store about 1930. The horse-drawn cart is advertising the unlikely combination of Cadbury's chocolate and Sunripe motorcars and cycles because Carter, Paterson and Co. was a road haulage company jointly owned by the so-called 'big four' railway companies including Southern Railway, which provided local deliveries of goods brought in by train.

Looking west, about 1920, with M. Davis' newsagent and tobacconist shop on the left, which continued as a business, albeit later sharing the premises with National Westminster Bank, until the 1990s.

HIGH STREET, BRASTED.

Pub by M. Davis, Brasted.

Looking east with Streatfield House, M. Davis' newsagent and tobacconist shop and the former butcher's shop in the foreground. The name of the house almost certainly refers to the Streatfield family who acquired Delaware, a large estate on the southern border of Brasted, in around 1700.

HIGH STREET, BRASTED

Looking east, 1951. The newsagent and tobacconist shopfront has now acquired two doors. In later years, the right-hand side of the shop was a sub-branch of National Westminster Bank in Westerham, also now closed. Watts' butcher shop closed in the 1990s and is now a house although the shopfront has been preserved.

Old Forge Cottages, 1911, which were sold at auction in 1912 when the Tipping estate was broken up. The house on the right of the row was a baker's shop until it closed for the last time in 1975.

Looking east, about 1905. The lime trees on the left beyond Tilings, still there today, look youthful. None of the shops can be clearly identified but the last incarnation of the shop furthest away on the right-hand side was as a hairdresser's and barber's shop before the shop extension was removed and the building converted into a house.

Brasted

Another view of the High Street from about 1905, looking east, with Tilings to the left, a scene that would be difficult to reproduce today bearing in mind the volume of traffic that passes this spot on a regular basis.

HIGH STREET, BRASTEAD, KENT

More or less the same scene some ten years later and an unusually busy looking High Street. Note again the introduction of telegraph poles in the intervening years.

Looking east, 1941. Lambert and Son's bakery at what is now Tilings is on the left. Daren bread was a style of bread, rich in wheat germ, containing increased levels of vital nutrients such as vitamin E.

Looking west, 1931, with the King's Arms on the right and the village petrol station on the left. Withers' Stores, with its prominent awning, is further along on the right.

Post Office, Brasted.

Withers' Stores, 1908, which was the village post office as well as a grocery and draper's shop. The goods on sale might have been even more diverse as garden spades are visible in the first floor, left-hand window. The shop sign refers to William Withers, who was succeeded as sub-postmaster in 1908 by John Sturge Withers.

Chartfield House. Note that, by the time this photograph was taken, it had undergone a mock Tudor transformation, acquired petrol pumps and become Bond's Garage, about 1930. The hanging sign states that they are an authorised dealer for Morris Cars.

Looking east, 1912. The entrance to Mill House is on the left but the row of buildings just beyond, including Fuggle's bakery, were all demolished to make way for a petrol station, which in turn gave way to a row of modern cottages.

The village hall, 1905 shortly after it was completed in 1900, funded by the widow of local philanthropist William Tipping who died in 1897. The hall was built on the site of an annual fair held on Ascension Day.

War Memorial, Brasted.

Looking east, 1941. Note the tablet on the war memorial contains only the fallen from the First World War and is therefore shorter than it is today, and the gates precede the present set, which were installed to commemorate the coronation of Queen Elizabeth II.

The Alms Row, Brasted.

The Stores, Brasted
W. Withers & Son

Alms Row looking west, 1911. Alms Row was built in the 16th century, part of which was in the style of a Wealden hall house, although it's not certain that was its original purpose, just visible behind the telegraph pole.

BRASTED. HIGH STREET.

Haynes Cottages in the foreground with Alms Row in the background looking east, about 1915. Number 10 at the far end of Alms Row is a mid-nineteenth century addition. Alms Row was acquired at auction and renovated by William Tipping shortly after he acquired Brasted Place.

Haynes Cottages, 1911, which were sold at auction, together with Alms Row, in 1912 when the Tipping estate was broken up.

Alms Row looking east, 1941, including the distinctive Wealden hall style house. Note the bus stop on the right, which was later moved to the junction of West End and the High Street.

The Bull Inn, about 1905. At this time, the Bull Inn was tied to Nalder and Collyer, a Croydon brewer, which was acquired by the City of London Brewery in 1919. The pub closed in 2011. The present building, on the corner of Church Road, dates from about this time, replacing a larger inn that stood on the site, previously known as the Black Bull Inn.

Heverswood Lodge, about 1950. Heverswood today is a modern house, built on the site of a nineteenth century house that was demolished in 1950, but it was originally part of the Hever Castle estate and was the site of a hunting lodge, which is thought to have been used by Henry VIII.

Annie Wells outside Alma House, which still stands opposite the former Bull Inn and is now known as Old Orchard. Annie ran a tea shop from the house with her sister Lily, but it was not a success. The Wells family owned a number of properties in Brasted.

Looking east with the village recreation ground on the left, 1919. The sign on the left says 'please drive slowly through this village' indicating that speeding traffic was already becoming a problem.

Home Farm, 1911, which was part of the Tipping Estate until it was sold at auction in 1912. Home Farm still operates today as a dairy farm.

Chapter 3

St Martin's Church and Church Road

Church Road runs north from the western end of the High Street, over the beautiful River Darent, past Mill Farm and the Stanhope Arms to St Martin's Church. After the church, the road continues on becoming Station Road north of the junction with Coles Lane.

There is archaeological evidence that a church existed in Brasted on the site of the current church in Saxon times and the church was mentioned in the Domesday Book of 1086. The church, which was gradually developed in mediaeval times, has a fascinating history and was extensively rebuilt in 1866. The church contains the Stocket Chapel which was originally the private family chapel of successive owners of Brasted Place, having been built in the early fourteenth century by the then owner, Simon de Stocket. The chapel survived the devastating fire that destroyed much of the church interior in 1989. Today, the names of all of those who fell in the First and Second World Wars are inscribed on the wooden panelling that adorns the chapel, which was restored in 2018 when names not originally included were added to the panelling.

It is thought that the centre of the village may once have been situated either around the church or between the church and the present-day Pilgrims Way, as the ground to the south of the church was marshy and prone to flooding. That, typically, churches are situated in the centre of their community while St Martin's is today situated on the northern edge of the village, also supports that assumption.

The Mill Pond, Brasted, Kent.

These two hand tinted cards together present a good panorama of Church Road beyond the River Darent and the millpond. Converted into a house in the 1960s, this corn mill still stands at the end of Mill Lane.

The Mill & Church, Brasted, Kent.

The earliest known reference to a mill on this site is dated 1867 although the present building is thought to date from 1881. It was operated by the Barton family from the mid nineteenth century up to the beginning of the First World War and it continued to be operational until the 1920s.

An unusual view of St Martin's looking across the fields to the west of Church Road with the North Downs in the distance, 1915.

Another unusual view of St Martin's with Church Road leading away from the High Street in the foreground, 1920.

Bull Cottages and the Baptist Chapel. Now a private house, the chapel was opened in 1866 and closed its doors for the last time after a carol service on 26th December 1989. The Manse in Coles Lane was the residence of the pastor.

Note the haystack in front of Mill Farm farmhouse! The clock on the south face of the church tower, a gift in memory of the late Richard T Durtnell from his widow, was installed in 1913.

The clock is absent in this photograph but the weathervane dates this as being after the church tower was restored in 1880. The cottages on the left housed a dame school, an early form of private elementary school, which was replaced by the National School in the High Street in 1860.

Slightly further back from the church, which has now acquired its tower clock. Mill Farm farmhouse, on the left, was built in 1702 and is named after one of two watermills that used to operate in the village. The former watermill still stands in the grounds of the farm, but it ceased operating about the end of the nineteenth century.

Church End House, on the left, was built in 1880 in the arts and crafts style and was the home of the Alderson family for many years. The Stanhope Arms is on the right.

Originally known as the Queen's Arms, the earliest known record of the Stanhope Arms is dated 1799, by which time the name had already changed to honour the 1st Earl Stanhope, a prominent military commander and statesman who died in 1721 and is buried at Chevening church.

A wedding party at the Stanhope Arms, probably about 1898 after Westerham brewer B C Bushell & Co. acquired Watkins and Son in 1897 and before acquiring George Smith and Co of Sevenoaks in 1899.

Parish Church, Brasted

This hand tinted card shows St Martin's and Church End House in about 1910. A V1 flying bomb landed in the field in the foreground in 1944, severely damaging the church.

St Martin's in 1909 predating the church car park, which now occupies the site to the right of this photo. The slightly shorter gable and smaller window on the left of the large altar window indicates the location of the choir vestry, which was added to the church in 1866. As well as serving as the choir vestry, this room is now also used for meetings and other gatherings.

A close up of the old lych gate, 1906. The lych gate was destroyed by a falling tree and was replaced by a replica in 2000.

St Martin's Church, about 1910. Originally a Saxon church, it was gradually rebuilt between the eleventh and thirteenth centuries. It was redesigned by the celebrated Victorian architect Alfred Waterhouse when it was substantially rebuilt in 1866. Note the haystack in the field, in what is now the church car park.

The earliest known photograph of St Martin's and, in fact, the earliest known photograph of Brasted, 1857, taken before the roof and the north and south walls were replaced to enlarge the church in 1866.

St Martin's following the 1866 rebuild, 1905. The memorial in the foreground is that of Francis Crawshay, who was a wealthy businessman from Wales who moved to Bradbourne House in Sevenoaks in 1867. The unusual design of the memorial stems from his interests in Druidism and seafaring.

St Martin's Church interior, March 1943. Note the chancel screen, the organ on the right-hand side and the screen to the left leading to the Stocket Chapel. In July 1944, a V1 flying bomb landed in the field to the east of the church, destroying the windows on that side, but worse was to come in November 1989, when a catastrophic fire destroyed the roof and much of the interior including the organ and the historic pulpit.

St Martin's Church interior, March 1943. Note the choir stalls are in the chancel. The chancel screen was removed in 1975. The choir stalls in the photograph were destroyed in the fire of 1989 and new choir stalls were re-sited in the nave as part of the restoration.

Chapter 4

Rectory Lane and Brasted Hill Road

Rectory Lane runs north from the centre of the High Street alongside the western edge of the village green, over the River Darent and steeply uphill where it becomes Brasted Hill Road, which climbs up to the Pilgrims Way and the North Downs. Two former rectories give this lane its name. The Old Rectory at the bottom of the hill dates from early Victorian times and was replaced as the rector's residence in 1940 by what is now The Chantry at the junction of Rectory Lane and Coles Lane. This residence, in turn, was replaced by the present Rectory in Coles Lane in 1979. To the north of this point, the lane becomes Brasted Hill Road.

R Durtnell and Sons, which was founded in 1591 and was Britain's oldest builder before their closure in 2019, were based in Rectory Lane as was the Durtnell family's home – Darenton - in the nineteenth century, which was later converted into flats. Durtnell's business premises extended either side of Rectory Lane, where The Old Yard, a group of modern small business units, and the dance school to the north of the river, now stand. The Old Forge, which stands on the road in front of the dance school and which was a workshop until the Second World War, indicates the former scale of Durtnell's business interests.

Further north, Tannery Cottages and Tanners, the latter hidden from the road by the escarpment to the east, bear witness to the existence of a tannery pond, which was situated to the east of the lane opposite the Old Rectory. The pond was filled in some time ago and two modern houses now stand on the site. The appearance of the escarpment on either side of the lane is as a result of quarrying in the nineteenth and earlier twentieth centuries. Tanners is the former home of Lord Nolan, who had a distinguished career in the legal profession and may be best known for his 1995 Report on Standards in Public Life.

RECTORY LANE, BRASTED.

Rectory Lane looking north from the bottom of the hill, about 1910. The entrance to what would have been the rector's residence when this photograph was taken, and is now known as the Old Rectory, is on the left.

Looking north, 1906. This distinctive bend in Rectory Lane is recognisable today with really only the lack of a tarmac surface indicating the age of the photograph.

Rectory Lane. Brasted

Looking north, 1904. The apparent erosion of the steep bank on either side of the lane, visible today, indicates the site of a former quarry.

Bowling Alley, about 1910, the local name for the footpath that joins Rectory Lane and Church Road. These distinctive steps at the Rectory Lane end of the path were replaced by concrete steps some time ago.

Rectory Lane, Brasted.

Published by The Stores
Brasted
W. Withers & Son.

Looking south towards Tannery Cottages, which were built in 1907. A pond stood to the left of the cottages, which is thought to have been used in the tanning process as hides were soaked in water to remove the salt left over from curing and to increase the moisture so that the hide or skin could be further treated.

Chapter 5

Brasted Chart and Toys Hill

Brasted Chart and Toys Hill are distinct and separate communities lying respectively about one mile and two and a half miles to the south of the village, with which they form the civil parish of Brasted. However, by a strange oddity, Toys Hill is in the ecclesiastical parish of neighbouring Sundridge with Ide Hill.

Toys Hill is situated on the Greensand Ridge overlooking the Weald of Kent. It is thought that Toys Hill took its name from a local land-owning family as Robert Toys is recorded as having paid 12d (twelve old pence) to the Manor of Otford in 1295 for the right to keep pigs in Otford Woods. Pig keeping was a major occupation in Brasted Chart when the area was primarily common land. Charcoal burning and quarrying for chert, a hard, fine-grained rock used for building and road surfacing at that time, were also significant industries on the Chart.

The majority of the houses, which are situated predominantly along Chart Lane, are relatively recent additions. Today, much of the land surrounding the two communities is owned by the National Trust, largely as a result of one of the Trust's founders, Octavia Hill, having lived at nearby Crockham Hill.

Brasted Chart was badly affected by the hurricane of October 1987 when many houses were damaged and thousands of trees were destroyed. Evidence of the hurricane can still be seen in the surrounding woodland today although the landscape has all but fully recovered, in part through some managed planting though mostly through natural regeneration.

The local postman delivering post to the cottages at the bottom of Chart Lane looking south, about 1920.

The bottom of Chart Lane looking south, 1912, a very recognisable scene more than a hundred years later.

STEPS TO BULL FIELDS, BRASTED. 396

Dated 1910, these steps still exist, from Chart Lane to the fields above, which extend almost to the High Street opposite what used to the Bull Inn. The fields may have been named after the livestock that may have been kept in them or because they belonged to the pub.

Colinette Cottages, 1906, tucked away about half a mile along an unadopted road off Chart Lane, were built in 1899 as part of the Colinette Farm estate.

The Star Inn, about 1950. Dartford Brewery, acquired by Style and Winch in 1924 who were later acquired by Barclay, Perkins and Co, was identified as a separate brand until the 1950s. The Star is now a private house.

The Fox and Hounds, 1908, two years after George Henry Moreton acquired the tenancy. The freehold was acquired by Westerham brewers Bushell and Co. in 1881.

The Fox and Hounds, perhaps in 1913 when Charles Partridge acquired the tenancy as his name is clearly visible on the hanging sign. A campaign to save the pub from closure ultimately failed when a planning appeal to convert it into a house was upheld in 2021.

The Tally Ho, Toys Hill, about 1910. As can be seen, the pub was tied at the time to Bushell, Watkins and Smith of Westerham. The Westerham brewers were acquired by Taylor, Walker and Co. in 1948. The Tally Ho is now a private house.

The Tally Ho, 1948, enjoyed a fine view from the Greensand Ridge over the Weald to the south, two of the most distinctive geological features in south-east England.

Puddledock Lane looking west, about 1910. Further along this lane is the distinctive roof of Toys Hill well. The well was sunk in 1898, funded by Crockham Hill resident Octavia Hill, a great social reformer and one of the founders of the National Trust.

Toys Hill village hall, about 1910. The hall, which was converted from an existing building in 1909, comprises both a hall and a chancel to enable the building to be used for religious services. Owen Fleming, who was responsible for building the Brasted swimming pool, gave fifty years' devoted service maintaining the hall.

View of the Weald to the south from Toys Hill village hall, about 1920. The distinctive seat in the foreground is still a prominent feature at the crossroads in the centre of Toys Hill.

View of the Weald from Toys Hill well and the look-out point, about 1920. The well would still have been in use as mains water was not installed for Toys Hill residents until the 1930s.

Scords Lane looking east with Toys Hill Farm oast in the distance, about 1910. Hops were the main crop around Toys Hill until the last hop garden was dug up in 1927.

Teachers and pupils of Toys Hill Farm School, about 1910. There is no information available about the school although the farmhouse, a late sixteenth century timber framed house with brick cladding from the eighteenth century is still a feature along Scords Lane

A Toys Hill cottage, later destroyed by a V1 Flying Bomb in 1943. Although V1s, launched from bases in the Pas de Calais, were designed to bomb London, many fell short of their target causing significant loss of life and damage in south-east London and Kent.

Chapter 6

The Big Houses

Two of the most significant houses in former times, Weardale Manor and Heverswood, were demolished respectively during the Second World War and in the immediate postwar period while Brasted Place and the Philippines have both been divided into apartments. Brasted Place was for a long time the home of the lord of the manor from at least the fourteenth century when the house was known as Stockets and situated closer to the High Street. Prominent former residents of the present house include Dr John Turton, physician to George III, and Prince Louis-Napoléon Bonaparte who later became Napoléon III of France. John Turton was responsible for rebuilding the house in the style that we see today, which was designed by Robert Adam, the great Georgian architect.

Later in the nineteenth century, the house was bought by the railway magnate William Tipping. Tipping deserves special mention as, according to a contemporary account, he 'found Brasted in a deplorable state, conspicuous for its poverty, its insanitary dwellings and its disreputable characters, including sheep stealers.' He became a great benefactor of the village improving the local roads and many cottages including Alms Row and contributing to the rebuilding of St Martin's Church and the railway from Westerham to Dunton Green. Brasted Place itself, previously in a neglected state, was repaired and, in 1871, extended with the addition of a west wing in French Renaissance style.

After the Tipping estate was broken up at auction in 1912, Brasted Place passed through various hands and was for a time an ecclesiastical college before it was divided into apartments in the 1990s.

Brasted Place in about 1920. Designed by Robert Adam for John Turton, physician to George III, this Palladian villa was built in 1784. A west wing, which can be seen on the left, in French Renaissance style was added by William Tipping in 1871. The original manor house, which can be traced back to the reign of Edward II, was sited closer to the main road when it was known as Stockets.

BRASTED PLACE, KENT

Brasted Place, about 1945. In 1840, it was briefly the home of Prince Louis-Napoléon Bonaparte who later became Napoléon III of France. William Tipping, who helped to fund many improvements in the village, bought Brasted Place in 1853 and lived there until his death in 1897. The 1871 extension can be clearly seen to the left of the main house in this photograph.

Brasted Place from the rockery, 1911, the year of the death of William Fearon Tipping, who had inherited the estate from his father in 1897.

The morning room, Brasted Place, 1911. These photographs were taken for the sale of the estate, which took place by auction in 1912.

Brasted Cross and bridge, standing in the grounds of Brasted Place. The bridge was part of the old Brasted to Ide Hill road, replaced by New Road, which was funded by Dr John Turton shortly after he acquired Brasted Place in 1784. The cross is believed to be a Saxon memorial commemorating a battle in 902 between the Danes and the Saxons, reputed to have taken place in Bloodins Field, north of Brasted on the North Downs ridge. The cross is now in private hands.

The Old Rectory, 1869, is early Victorian. It was replaced as the rector's residence in 1940 by what is now The Chantry at the junction of Rectory Lane and Coles Lane, and that in turn was replaced by the present Rectory in Coles Lane in 1979.

Church End House, 1911, which was part of the Tipping estate until it was bought at auction in 1912 by George Alderson, for many years the owner of a major transport company based in Brasted.

Weardale Manor.

Published by
The Stores. Brasted
W. Withers & Son.

Built in 1906, Weardale Manor was the home of Philip Stanhope, 1st Baron Weardale and his wife, Countess Alexandra Tolstoy. It was occupied only in the summer months. After Philip Stanhope died in 1923, Lady Weardale rarely visited the house and, on her death, she left it to her nephew, 7th Earl Stanhope. Lacking the funds to maintain it, the house was demolished in 1939. The foundations and terrace are all that remain.

The Phillipines, Brasted.

The Stores. Brasted
W. Withers & Son.

Philippines is sometimes a difficult word to spell, even on a postcard, although the connection with the islands in the South China Sea is uncertain. Built in 1834 for Thomas Bignold, it was later occupied by Joshua Wilson Faulkner, a well-known portrait miniaturist. Later converted to a care home, it was divided into apartments and, together with surrounding new-build houses, is now known as Ide Hill Park.

Brasted, Heverswood S. Front.

Heverswood was originally part of the Hever Castle estate and was the site of a hunting lodge, which is thought to have been used by Henry VIII.

Heverswood, Brasted.

Heverswood, as seen here, was a substantial property built in the nineteenth century, occupied at one time by George Henderson, a prominent Scottish East India Company merchant. It was used as a military convalescent home during and after the Second World War.

Heverswood fell into disrepair in the post-war period and was demolished in 1950. It was replaced by a smaller house although the original nineteenth century cellar survives.

Vines Gate is one of the oldest houses on the Chart as it dates back four hundred years when it was originally a Huguenot farmhouse and part of the Brasted Place estate. It was purchased from the estate in the 1840s when it was enlarged to take on its present-day appearance.

Foxwold Chase, now known simply as Foxwold, was completed in 1885 for Horatio Noble Pym, a London lawyer and so named because his wife's maiden name was Fox. The house and estate remained in the Pym family until the house was sold in 2001. Foxwold and its grounds were used in location scenes in the 1985 Merchant Ivory film 'A Room with A View'.

Village House, decorated to celebrate the coronation of Queen Elizabeth II in 1953. This Georgian house is in a prominent position in the centre of the High Street. At the back of the house, there are indications of an earlier seventeenth century house.

Chapter 7
The Railway

The Westerham Valley Railway, which ran between Westerham and Dunton Green, was opened in July 1881. William Tipping and Richard Durtnell jointly guaranteed the sum of £50,000 to enable the necessary private bill to be passed through Parliament in 1876. In their submission, representatives of the new railway stated that the turnpike road from Westerham to Sevenoaks was very narrow and that "the brewers with their large wagons were always on it." They also stated that the only public means of transport from Westerham to Sevenoaks was an omnibus, which ran twice a day and took three hours to cover the distance of six miles because it stopped "at every public house on the road."

Local businesses, including R Durtnell and Son, Westerham Brewery and George Alderson's coal yard, benefited greatly from the railway while passengers were able to use the initial nine return journeys on weekdays with six on Sundays. By 1938, this had increased to 22 trains each way on weekdays, 21 on Saturdays and 18 down and 17 up trains on Sundays. The journey from Westerham to London took around ninety minutes but, after timetable changes, this was reduced to a little over an hour.

However, with increasing car ownership and the introduction of a reliable bus service to Sevenoaks, whose station provided better connections to London, the line started to run at a loss despite successive cuts to running costs in the postwar period. The line was closed in October 1961 although the tracks and even the station survived until 1977 when construction of the M25 began. The inside lane of the westbound carriageway marks the site of the old railway line as it ran from east to west through Brasted.

The former approach road to the station still exists exactly as it was as does the former stationmaster's house. A service gate onto the westbound carriageway of the M25 marks the spot where the station building stood.

Looking east towards Sevenoaks. Brasted station master Mr. E.W. Howard with two of his staff about 1912. The line between Westerham and Dunton Green was single track and Brasted station comprised a single platform on the south side of the track. Note the signal box in the distance on the left-hand side of the track.

Stationmaster Mr Howard with what today would seem like a large complement of staff for a small village station. Brasted lost its station master in 1924 and, from then on, the station was managed from Dunton Green.

The train, known as the Westerham Flyer, leaves Brasted station heading towards Westerham, 1961. The village lies beyond the railway bridge, which was replaced in 1977 by a road bridge carrying the new M25 over Station Road at this point.

The same railway bridge looking in the opposite direction. Note the station sign on the right at the entrance to the approach road to the station.

The Westerham Flyer approaches Brasted station from Westerham heading towards Dunton Green, 1953.

The station name and 'SR' for Southern Railway picked out in stones, and the attractive floral display, evidently taken from the train, were on the opposite side of the track from the single platform.

The station looking west, June 1960. In 1955, the branch line was reported to be losing £11,600 per month and, to reduce costs, staff were withdrawn and the station was re-named and re-signed Brasted Halt.

Brasted Halt on 28th October 1961, the penultimate day before the line closed. Although the line was subsequently purchased by a steam railway preservation society, the bid to re-open the line as a heritage line ultimately failed.

The photographer was evidently able to climb down from the platform and walk across the track to take this photograph of the same train before health and safety was invented!

The Westerham Flyer makes its last journey on 29th October 1961 when the branch line was closed, not by Dr Beeching as many think but by the then Minister of Transport, Ernest Marples.

The station building in 1962, which was disused by this time. The building survived in a semi-derelict state until 1977 when it was demolished to make way for the new M25. A service gate leading onto the motorway now stands on this spot.

Chapter 8

Village Life

Brasted was fairly self-sufficient in providing almost anything that people might want to buy and in terms of employment and business opportunities. In common with many smaller communities at that time, most people were born, went to school, worked and raised families here rarely relocating outside the immediate area. Even travel to the nearby towns of Oxted and Sevenoaks was relatively rare until the advent of wider ownership of private transport.

All of these factors combined to create the conditions for a much closer knit community than we are used to in modern life, evident in many of these photographs. The village school did much to foster a strong sense of community as the school taught local children from their early years to school leaving age. After the Second World War, the new Churchill School opened in nearby Westerham for children aged eleven and above and Brasted School continued as a primary school until its closure in 1988.

Many Brasted people worked locally on the farms, in the shops or in the many local businesses, which included the building trade, haulage, the carriage works and several forges. Brasted also had a thriving social life centred around the two churches, seven pubs and the village halls in Brasted village and Toys Hill, both of which hosted regular and varied events.

The swimming pool at the village recreation ground, which opened in 1914, was a popular attraction, bringing in people from far and wide, even if bathers found the river-fed pool was always cold and contained local aquatic wildlife! The pool declined in popularity and closed in 1953 amid concerns about the possible contamination of one of the springs feeding it.

Brasted School children, 1898. Top row, left to right, Mr T Hubble (schoolmaster), G. Hills, G Palmer, W Young, J Pattenden, B Curtis, C Parrett; second row, B Ford, G Long, F Hills, E Cowlard, A Wells, L Muddle, C Waters; third row, A King, M Cronk, E Davey, R Mitchell, E Parrett, S Russell; bottom row, C Cronk, B Alderson, W Muddle.

"VILLAGE SCHOOL, BRASTED."   Pub. by M. Davis, Brasted.   [Entered at Stationers' Hall]

Brasted School children, 1907. The school, which opened in 1860, closed in 1988 when it amalgamated with Sundridge School. The building served as a temporary church following the fire at St Martin's in 1989 before conversion to private houses and a doctor's surgery in 1992.

Boys at Brasted School, about 1920, practising their horticultural skills at the back of the school, an important lesson as farming was still a major local source of employment at the time.

Girls at Brasted School, about 1920, at an outdoor cookery lesson, another important subject bearing in mind that convenience foods and ready meals were still a long way into the future. Proudly overseeing the class is Headmaster Thomas Hubble, who had been both a pupil and pupil teacher at the school. He was appointed headteacher in 1888 at the age of 21, a position he was to hold until December 1919. He actively fostered a close relationship between the village and the school and was very understanding of the demands that country life placed on his pupils at key times in the farming calendar, such as at harvest time.

Hop pickers at Toys Hill, 1912. Historical records show that hop farming was widespread in the local area and there is still evidence of that today in the form of the oast houses in Elliotts Lane and at Outridge Farm, and wild hop vines growing in some of the hedgerows.

Frank Williams and family outside Brasted Hall, 1903. Frank Williams generously donated a new organ for St Martin's Church in 1906 and a house, the Manse in Coles Lane, for the minister of Brasted Baptist Church.

The Pym family pose in the Foxwold library during a fancy dress ball in 1909. Back row, Alwyn Ball (third left), Edmund Ball (extreme right) and at the front, Sylvia Pym (third left seated), Hannah Pym (fourth left standing), Elfrida Ball (fifth left seated), Arnold Ball (sixth left standing) and Stella Pym (seventh left seated).

Arch Day with his son, Reg, about 1950. Arch took over the tenancy of the dairy at Mill Farm with his two brothers, Fred and Henry, in 1934 where the brothers' father, Harry, had previously been a stockman, renting the farm from the Chevening Estate. He continued to supply milk to the local area until 1969.

R Durtnell and Son's annual staff outing, about 1890, in front of Darenton, the Durtnell family home on the village green. Annual staff outings were a tradition in many companies well into the twentieth century.

Owen Fleming of Toys Hill conducting a preliminary dig for the new Darenth Valley Swimming Bath, to give it its original official title, 1913. Mr Fleming chose the site, adjacent to the River Darent in the village recreation ground, to use the river water to feed the pool. Note St Martin's Church in the background.

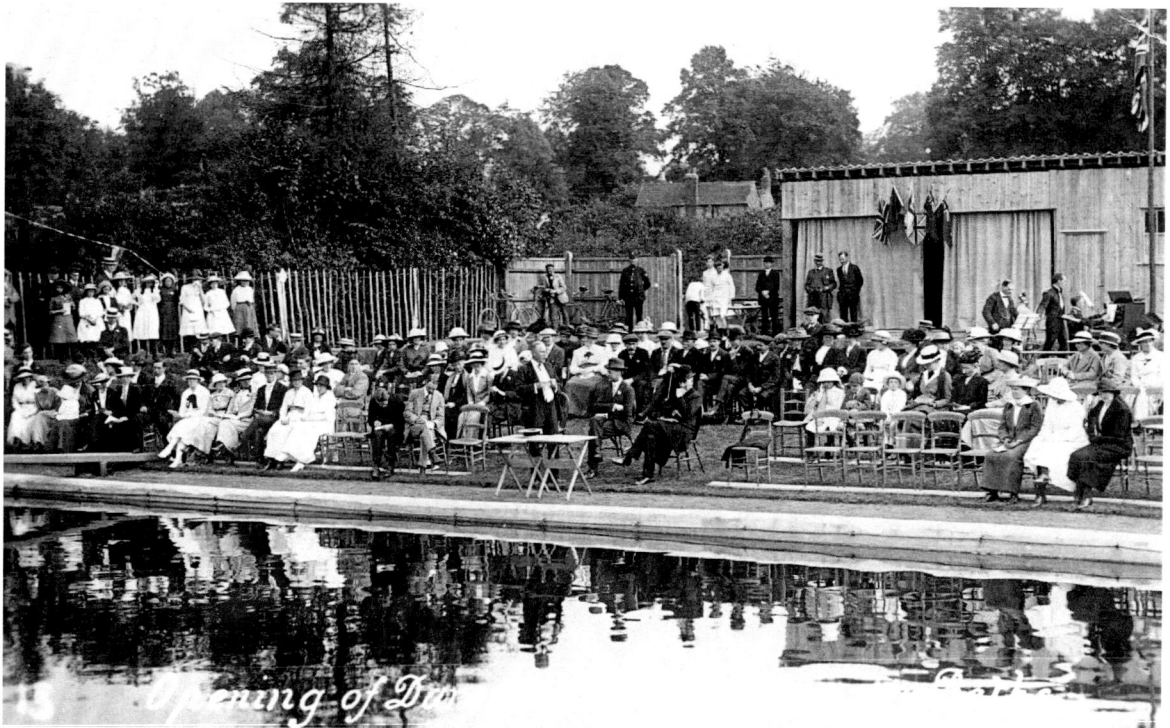

The swimming bath was opened on 24th June 1914 to great ceremony, which included a torchlight procession from Brasted village green to Westerham comprising various local associations including the Westerham Town Band and the 4th West Kent Territorials.

Swimmers and spectators enjoy the evident sunshine and warmth at the swimming bath, about 1930, at the height of its popularity.

On the site of the present tennis courts, the pool was very popular drawing people to Brasted from the wider area by train and bus.

George Alderson's fleet of horse-drawn wagons lines up behind Church End House, probably in 1920 when he decided to retire his fleet of horse-drawn wagons, replacing them with motorised transport for his coal and haulage businesses.

In 1921, he moved into coach travel. His son, also George, inherited the business in 1946 and, by 1960, he had disposed of the coal and haulage businesses continuing to operate his coach fleet until he retired in 1965.

Pharaoh Burgess (right) outside his son-in-law Dick Turner's hardware shop. The shop is now the village store. Pharaoh Burgess was Honorary Secretary and Chairman of the Sundridge and Brasted Horticultural Society helping to re-start the Society after the Second World War.

Brasted Cricket Club, 1910, probably taken at Piper's Green, where the club still plays its home matches today.

Brasted and Sundridge FC, 1913-14 season, a poignant image bearing in mind what was to come. The trophy on the left is the Sevenoaks Charity Senior Cup, which began in 1894 and is one of the oldest football competitions in England.

Brasted and Sundridge FC, 1921-22 season. Following the First World War, Sevenoaks and District Football League was reformed in 1920, sufficient clubs having joined to enable two divisions to run.

Brasted Carnival procession, celebrating Queen Victoria's diamond jubilee, June 1897. The carnival was a major annual event in which almost everyone in Brasted took part in one way or another.

'The Queen Mary' float for the Brasted Carnival with, left to right, George Brown and Bill Annells, May 1935. Mill House, still standing, is just visible on the left, and Fuggle's bakery chimney, later demolished, is on the right.

The Bull inn, 1950, still bearing its Nalder's livery, although Nalder and Collyer had been acquired by the City of London Brewery in 1919 who ended their association with brewing in 1968. The Bull was sold to Shepherd Neame who kept the pub until it was sold for development in 2011.

Procession in the High Street, with Tilings and Old Forge Cottages clearly visible in the background, celebrating the coronation of George VI in May 1937.

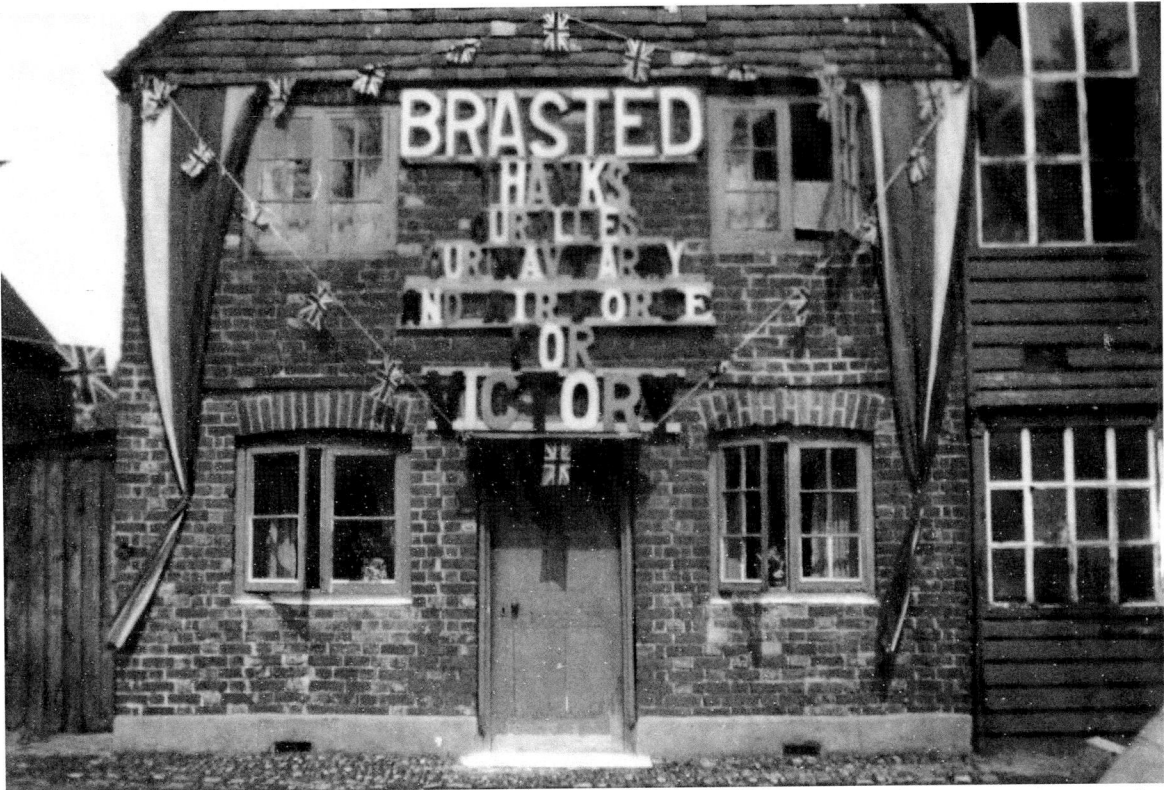

Mrs Emily Bailey of 7, The Green, Brasted celebrated the end of World War 2 on Victory in Europe Day (VE Day) 8th May 1945. The message reads, 'Brasted Thanks Our Allies Our Navy Army and Air Force for Victory'. The old wheelwright's shop is just visible on the right.

Demolishing the communal air raid shelter on the green, March 1948. The outline of the foundations of the shelter can be seen through the grass on the green during spells of very dry weather.

The 7th Earl Stanhope unveiling the new village sign on the green, 1951. The sign depicts the Pilgrims' Way and the Archbishop's Garden, which comprises of the parishes of Brasted, Chevening and Sundridge.

A mock court leet, 1952. A court leet is a criminal court dating back to mediaeval times. Teddy Preston, the publican at the White Hart, volunteered to be in the dock charged with 'selling sour and musty beer'. He was acquitted. Note the windowless building in the background, which was the village morgue and has since been used as a shop, variously a general store, pottery workshop and coffee shop with varying success.

The bell ringing team at St Martin's, including Cornet Davy, Thomas Dunn, Robert Howell, Billy Parrett and Jack Wells, 1908. Sadly, we don't know who is who.

Brasted Mothers' Union, about 1940. From left to right, Mrs Carter, Mrs Waggoner, Mrs Theobold, Mrs Greenaway, Mrs Budgen, Mrs Longuet-Higgins, Mrs Cramp, Mrs Fry, Mrs Clout, Miss Hollamby, Mrs Forester, Mrs Still, Mrs Swift, Mrs Cole, Mrs Towner, and Mrs Gowlett.

Lewis Watts in his shop, 1950. Brasted was still fairly self-sufficient in terms of shopping for everyday goods until the late 1970s.

An impressive Christmas display, 1950. Lewis Watts' shop, with its distinctive decoration and butcher's hooks still above the window, is still identifiable in the High Street today.

Chapter 9

Brasted Miscellany

Many interesting items of local ephemera have survived the years providing an interesting insight into life in Brasted as it was in the nineteenth and early twentieth centuries.

Old business receipts and advertisements tell us something about the businesses that existed here and the wide variety of goods and services they offered. Even as recently as the 1970s, High Street shops still included grocery, baker's, chemist's, greengrocer's, tobacconist and newsagent's, butcher's and hairdresser's and barber's shop, a haberdashery, a bank and a post office.

Various posters and programmes tell us about the entertainment and other activities that people living in Brasted enjoyed, including regular dances held in the village hall and the hall adjacent to the swimming pool, where the village recreation ground pavilion now stands. The annual Brasted Carnival and participation in national events, such as coronations, were evidently very popular events and well supported by people in Brasted.

Other items of ephemera bear witness to some of the landmark events that took place in Brasted, such as the auction held in the village hall in 1912 at which the extensive Tipping estate was sold and broken up. Orders of service remind us of the dedication of the memorial in the Stocket Chapel in 1919, which had previously been a private chapel in St Martin's Church to commemorate the tragic loss of so many of Brasted's young men in the First World War, as well as the unveiling of the war memorial in the High Street in 1919, extended in 1948 to accommodate the names of those lost in the Second World War.

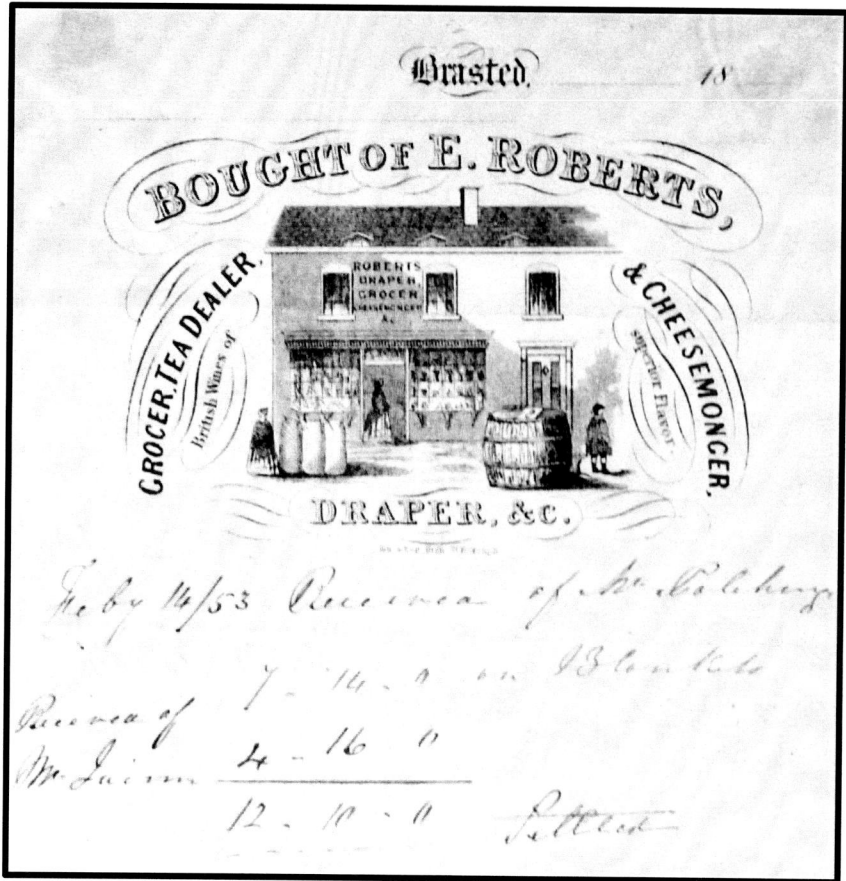

They don't make shop receipts like this any more! A receipt for 21 blankets at 12s 6d (62.5p) each, nearly a weekly wage for an agricultural labourer at the time, purchased by Brasted Eleemosynary Charities in March 1851 for the poor of Brasted. The Charities, which comprise of four bequests, the earliest of which dates back to 1638, have been providing support to people in need in Brasted ever since, an astonishing example of continuity in local charitable work.

Another receipt for blankets for Brasted Charities to be given to the poor. Dated April 1858, this shows the blankets cost 13s (65p) each. The charitable gifts that were given away by Brasted Eleemosynary Charities in the nineteenth century help us to understand how precarious life was for many people in Brasted. As wells as blankets, gifts often included boots, bales of cloth for making clothes and sacks of coal, donations that we would more likely associate with some of the poorest third world countries today.

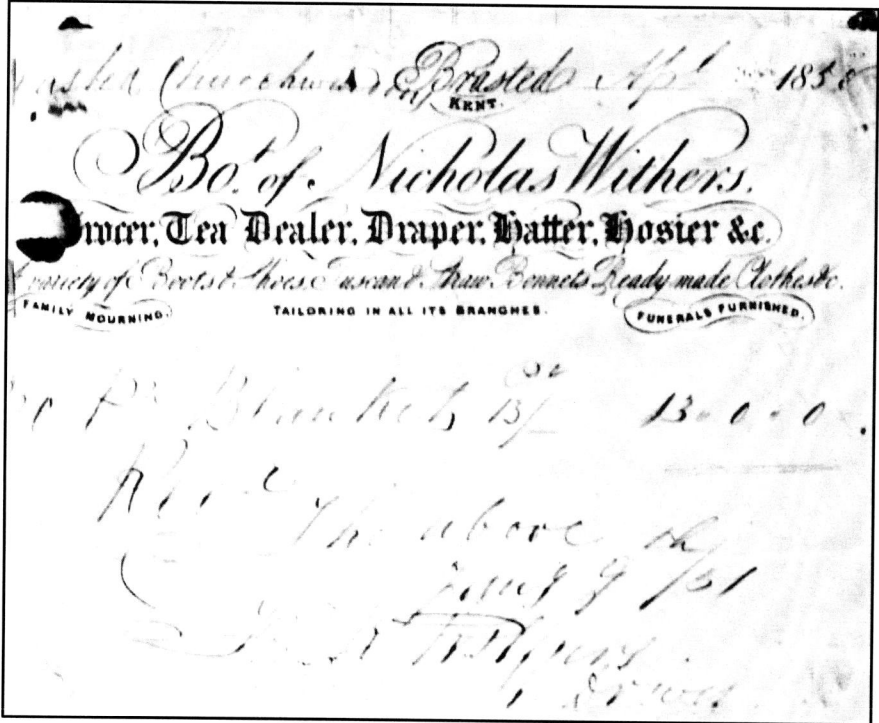

O, J. WOODHAMS,
FAMILY GROCER,
BRASTED.

Begs to call attention to his new stock of

BENZOLINE AND PARRAFFINE
LAMPS !

Which comprises several handsome and useful patterns.

Parraffine Lamps and Glass from 1/- each.

Benzoline   ditto   ,,   6d.   ,,

A reminder of a time before electricity was supplied to Brasted when paraffin lamps were the only source of lighting other than candles.

CHANGE OF ADDRESS.

G. ALDERSON,

BEGS to inform his customers that he has given up the license of the Bull Inn, Brasted, and has removed to

CHURCH END, BRASTED,

where he will continue to carry on the business of

COAL & COKE MERCHANT,
—— JOB MASTER, and ——
MOTOR CAR PROPRIETOR,

First-Class Open and Closed Motors FOR HIRE.	THE COAL, COKE & FORAGE MERCHANT.

RING UP NO. **4** BRASTED.

Telegrams : " Alderson, Brasted."

An advertisement from George Alderson announcing his move from the Bull Inn to Church End House in 1918 after he had acquired it from the Tipping estate six years earlier.

C. CHANDLER & SONS

BRASTED PREMISES.

GROCERS, DRAPERS,

— AND —

GENERAL WAREHOUSEMEN,

BRASTED AND OXTED.

An advertisement featuring a photograph of Chandler & Sons' premises, close to the junction of Rectory Lane, which will be familiar to most people in Brasted as the shopfront is almost identical today and was for many years known as Markwick's Stores.

By direction of H. AVRAY TIPPING, Esq.

KENT

Between Sevenoaks and Westerham

The Beautiful Freehold and Residential Estate

KNOWN AS

BRASTED PLACE

Situate in the pretty Kentish Village of Brasted, about one mile from the Station, four miles from Sevenoaks, two miles from Westerham, and extending to about

650 ACRES

Mostly in Brasted Parish, but partly in that of Sundridge, including

The MANSION, standing in a finely timbered Park of 120 Acres and containing six Reception Rooms, 22 Bed and Dressing Rooms, two Bathrooms, Stabling for seven horses, Motor House, etc., Model Home Farm, and Beautiful Old Gardens.

Also 18-HOLE GOLF COURSE has been planned under the advice of James Braid. Home Farm and densely timbered Woodlands. Several excellent Private Residences, Village Shops, Water Mill, and numerous Cottages, which

Messrs. KNIGHT, FRANK & RUTLEY

have been instructed to offer by Auction as a whole, or in Lots, on TUESDAY, 11th JUNE, 1912, at THE VILLAGE HALL, BRASTED, commencing at TWO o'clock precisely (unless previously sold by Private Treaty).

Solicitors :	*Auctioneers & Land Agents :*
Messrs. CORBOULD, RIGBY & Co.	Messrs. KNIGHT, FRANK & RUTLEY
1, HENRIETTA STREET	20, HANOVER SQUARE, LONDON, W.,
CAVENDISH SQUARE, LONDON, W	*Who will issue Orders to View*

Poster announcing the sale by auction of the Brasted Place Estate in 1912 following the death of William Fearon Tipping. Photographs of parts of the estate, taken from the auction catalogue, appear elsewhere in this book.

PROGRAMME

OF

CONCERT

IN AID OF

The · Brasted · Bathing · Pool.

18th JUNE. 1913.

Hooker Brothers, Printers, Westerham.

PROGRAMME.

TRIOS ... ... (a) Gavotte ... ... *Rameau.*
... ... (b) Serenade ... ... *Widor.*
MRS. SCOTT ARNOTT, MISS PHYLLIS HASLUCK,
MR. W. A. TAYLOR.

SONG ... "When May and June were wed" *Marie Warden*
MISS ISMAY TRIMBLE.

SONGS ... ... (a) "To Mary" *M. V. White.*
... (b) "The Gentle Maiden" *Irish Traditional.*
MR. FREDRICK KEEL.

'CELLO SOLOS ... (a) Siciliano .. *Pergolese.*
(b) Allegro Appassionata *Saint Säens.*
MISS PHYLLIS HASLUCK.

SONG ... "Four Jolly Sailormen" *Ed. German.*
"MR. FRANCES DRAKE," A.B.

VIOLIN SOLOS (a) Mazurka ... *Wienaiwshi.*
... (b) La Precieuse ... *Couperin-Kreisler.*
MRS. SCOTT ARNOTT.

SONG ... ... "Roundelay" ... *C. A. Lidgey.*
MISS ELIZABETH CURRIE.

RECITATION
"The Cricket Club of Rednose Flat" *J. Hickory Wood.*
MR. ALFRED BECK.

'CELLO SOLOS (a) Herbst Blume .. *Popper.*
... (b) Am Springbrunnen ... *Davidoff.*
MISS PHYLLIS HASLUCK.

SONG ... ...
"MR. FRANCES DRAKE," A.B.

SONG ... "Where my Caravan has rested" *Herman Löhr.*
MISS ELIZABETH CURRIE.

SONGS ... (a) "My Sweet Sweeting" *Fred Keel.*
(b) "Dabbling in the Dew" *Folk Song arr. by Cecil Sharp.*
MR. FREDRICK KEEL.

VIOLIN SOLO Tambourin Chinois ... *Kreisler.*
MRS. SCOTT ARNOTT.

SONG ... "The time to Smile" *Jean Bohannan.*
MISS ISMAY TRIMBLE.

TWO FISHING SONGS (a) "The Three Anglers"
(b) "Little Willie Brown"
MR. ALFRED BECK.

TRIOS ... Two Hungarian Dances *Brahms-Joachim.*
MRS. SCOTT ARNOTT, MISS PHYLLIS HASLUCK,
MR. W. A. TAYLOR.

"GOD SAVE THE KING."

⬧ INTERVAL ⬧
During which Mr. OWEN FLEMING will explain the plan of the Bathing Pool.

A 1913 programme for a concert at the village hall to raise funds for the building of the new swimming bath.

Dareηth Valley Swimming Bath.

(Adjoining BRASTED RECREATION GROUND).

President:
EARL STANHOPE.

Committee of Management:
J. S. MARRIOTT, *Chairman.*

SCOTT ARNOTT (*Hon. Solicitor*).   ERNEST DOWSING.
RAYMOND BUSH.   OWEN FLEMING (*Hon. Architect*).
SIDNEY BUTTERFIELD.   THOS. HUBBLE.
HOWARD RUSSELL.

Contractors:
MR. PETER BOTTING.   MESSRS. HORTON & SON.

Swimming Instructor & Superintendent:
G. ROBINSON, late R.M.L.I.

PROGRAMME
OF

Opening Ceremony
ON

JUNE 24th, 1914,

At 3.30 p.m.

Price 1d.

TORCHLIGHT PROCESSION.

At 9 p.m. a Torchlight Procession will form up in Rectory Lane, Brasted, and will march from Brasted Green to Westerham Green. On arrival at Westerham Green, the Band and Territorials will proceed to the centre of the Green and countermarch while the remainder of the Procession will surround the Green. The 10.33 p.m. Train from Westerham to Dunton Green will be strengthened to carry 300 passengers. There will however be no special connection from Dunton Green to Sevenoaks.

ORDER OF PROCESSION.

Screen of Cyclists
(Under the direction of Lieut. Eustace Marriott).

Advanced Guard of Brasted Athletic Club
(Under the direction of Mr. Owen Fleming).

Westerham Town Band
(Bandmaster - Mr. A. E. Newton).

4th West Kent Territorials
Westerham and Sundridge Company (Commanded by Capt. Cohen).
Sevenoaks Company (Commanded by Capt. Norman Smithers).

Westerham and Chipstead Cadets
(Commanded by Major P. W. Beresford).

Westerham Fire Brigade
(Capt. C. W. Hooker).

Combe Bank Fire Brigade
(Capt. H. Moore).

Association of Football Clubs
(Under the direction of Mr. W. H. Chase).

Screen of Cyclists
(Under the direction of Mr. Raymond Bush).

GOD SAVE THE KING.

HOOKER BROS., WESTERHAM.

The programme for the opening ceremony of the swimming bath in 1914 which included a marching band and torchlight procession.

BRASTED SWIMMING POOL

A NATURAL SPRING WATER POOL

Length 75 feet.   Breadth 50 feet.   Depth 3 to 7 feet

Water Chute,   Spring Boards,   Running 6ft. Dive and 12ft. Dive

MIXED BATHING is permitted, and the bath will be open (except in bad weather, when the flag is not flown) as follows :

WEEK DAYS	10 a.m. to 1 p.m. ;	2.30 p.m. to 7.30 p.m.
	No admission after 12	No admission after 7 p.m.
SUNDAYS	11 a.m. to 1 p.m. ;	3 p.m. to 5.30 p.m.
	No admission after 12	No admission after 5 p.m.

PRICES OF ADMISSION.

For Residents of Brasted and the immediate neighbourhood

WEEK DAYS	ADULTS	- - -	6d.
	do.	After 5 p.m.	3d.
	CHILDREN (14 and under) -		3d.
	do.	After 5 p.m.	2d.
SUNDAYS Morning	ADULTS - - -		1/-
	CHILDREN - - -		6d.
Afternoon	ADULTS - - -		3d.
	CHILDREN - - -		2d.

For Non-Residents

ALL DAYS	ADULTS - - -		1/-
	CHILDREN (14 and under) -		6d.

COSTUMES can be hired for 5d. and TOWELS for 2d.

SEASON TICKETS (which must be shown on application) as follows :—

FAMILY TICKETS of £1 1s. admit all members of a family.

SINGLE TICKETS 5s.   Children under 14, 2/6.

Non-Residents

FAMILY TICKETS £2 2s. admit all members of a family.

SINGLE TICKETS 10s.   Children under 14, 5s.

SPECIAL TERMS for Schools, Boy Scouts, on application.

Spectators Half-price.

Opening times and prices of admission for Brasted swimming pool, 1940. The pool was filled in, in part with the demolished changing rooms and adjacent pavilion, when the present pavilion and tennis courts were built in 1991.

BRASTED SWIMMING BATH.
DANCING ENTERTAINMENT.
August 5th, 6 p.m.

PROGRAMME.

PART I.

1. Six Country Dances - Brasted Folk Dancing Class
    - (a) Gathering Peascods.
    - (b) Rufty-Tufty.
    - (c) Mage on a Cree.
    - (d) Black-Nag.
    - (e) Jenny Pluck Pears.
    - (f) Bo-peep.

2. Quadrilles in Costumes.

SHORT INTERVAL.

PART II.

3. Minuet - - - Members of Rest Club

4. Duet - - - ,, ,,

5. Flamborough Sword Dance - Brasted Athletic Club.

6. Gavotte - - - Members of Rest Club

7. "Narcissus" - - Members of Rest Club

8. Lancers in Costume.

9. Kirby Sword Dance - - Brasted Athletic Club

Bijou Orchestra.

HOOKER BROS., WESTERHAM.

A programme for an evening's entertainment at Brasted swimming bath. The Flamborough and Kirby sword dances are marginally less dangerous than they sound as they were traditional dances originating from Yorkshire performed with wooden staves.

Parish Church of S. Martin,

BRASTED.

✠

Dedication of the Stocket Chapel, set apart

to the memory of Brasted men and others

connected with the parish, who fell in the

Great War, by the Right Reverend the

• • Lord Bishop of Rochester • •

✠

Thursday, July 24th, 1919,

Eve of the feast of S. James.

8 p.m.

The front cover of the order of service for the dedication of the Stocket Chapel War Memorial in St Martin's Church in 1919. The chapel had previously been the private chapel of the owners of Brasted Place but, when Leslie Urquhart bought the house at auction in 1912, he decided to sell the chapel. In 1919, it was bought on behalf of an anonymous benefactor on behalf of Brasted for use as a war memorial.

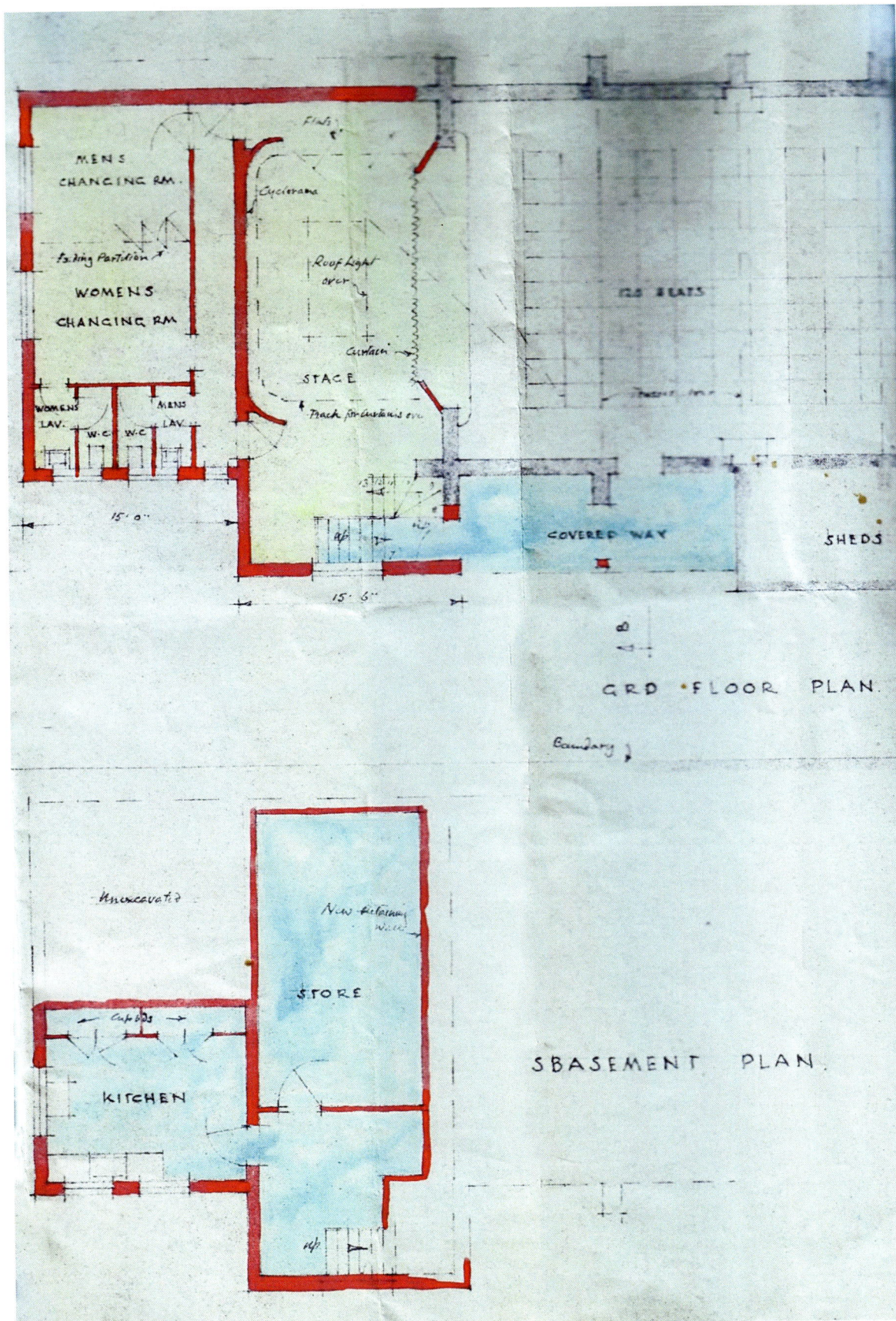

MENS CHANGING RM.

Flies

Cyclorama

Folding Partition

WOMENS CHANGING RM.

Roof Light over

Curtain

STAGE

WOMENS LAV.

W.C W.C

MENS LAV.

Track for curtains over

15'0"

15'6"

120 SEATS

COVERED WAY

SHEDS

GRD FLOOR PLAN.

Boundary

Unexcavated

New Retaining Wall

STORE

Cupbds

KITCHEN

SBASEMENT PLAN.

Part of the plans for an extension to the village hall, 1939. The plans were ambitious and included the building of a large extension at the rear to accommodate a new stage with male and female dressing rooms to the rear and an underground kitchen and storeroom. The existing stage was to be replaced with a foyer and bar but, in the event, only the modest two storey extension that we see today was built.

111

BRASTED
VICTORY MEMORIAL

To commemorate those who gave their lives

in the Second World War

1939—1945

and the Victory of the United Nations

UNVEILING AND DEDICATION
ON
SUNDAY, 11th JULY, 1948

---

3 o'clock in the High Street opposite the War Memorial.

Unveiling by MAJOR C. E. PYM, C.B.E., D.L., J.P., of the names of those who gave their lives in the Second World War.

Dedication by the Rector of the Parish, the REV. HUGH LONGUET LONGUET-HIGGINS.

Wreaths will be laid by MRS. SCOTT ARNOTT and the BRITISH LEGION.

The Last Post and Reveille.

BRITISH LEGION TRUMPETERS.

The Company will move to the Recreation Ground in the Westerham Road.

Address by MR. GILBERT J. M. LONGDEN, Chairman of the Brasted Victory Memorial Committee.

Official Opening of the Memorial Ground by MAJOR C. E. PYM, C.B.E., D.L., J.P.

MR. GEOFFREY D. DURTNELL will receive the ground on behalf of the Parish Council.

Dedication Service to be conducted by the Rector.

HYMN NO. 298 (A. & M.)

PRAISE, my soul, the King of Heaven,
To His feet thy tribute bring ;
Ransom'd, heal'd, restored, forgiven,
Evermore His praises sing ;
Alleluia ! Alleluia !
Praise the everlasting King.

Father-like, He tends and spares us,
Well our feeble frame He knows ;
In His hands He gently bears us,
Rescues us from all our foes ;
Alleluia ! Alleluia !
Widely yet His mercy flows.

Praise Him for His grace and favour
To our fathers in distress ;
Praise Him still the same as ever,
Slow to chide and swift to bless ;
Alleluia ! Alleluia !
Glorious in His faithfulness.

Angels in the height, adore Him ;
Ye behold Him face to face ;
Saints triumphant, bow before Him,
Gather'd in from every race ;
Alleluia ! Alleluia !
Praise with us the God of grace. Amen.

THE LESSON, Ch. 11 verse 33 to Ch. 12 verse 2 from the Epistle to the Hebrews will be read by MR. ROBERT EARL.

PRAYERS.

HYMN NO. 379 (A. & M.)

NOW thank we all our God,
With heart, and hands, and voices,
Who wondrous things hath done,
In whom His world rejoices ;
Who from our mother's arms
Hath bless'd us on our way
With countless gifts of love,
And still is ours today.

O may this bounteous God
Through all our life be near us,
With ever joyful hearts
And blessed peace to cheer us ;
And keep us in His grace,
And guide us when perplex'd,
And free us from all ills
In this world and the next.

All praise and thanks to God
The Father now be given,
The Son, and Him Who reigns
With them in highest Heaven,
The One Eternal God,
Whom earth and Heav'n adore,
For thus it was, is now,
And shall be evermore. Amen.

GOD SAVE THE KING.

Names of the Fallen
1939 - 1945

DAVID SCOTT ARNOTT
ANTHONY BARKER
FREDERICK BRETT
LAWRENCE CHESSON
HENRY PATRICK COBB
RONALD DINGWALL
HARRY DILGERT
JAMES GROVE
CHARLES HILLS
BARBARA LEWIS
JOHN LEWIS
RICHARD LONG
DEREK CHARLES McCAW

The unveiling and dedication of the Brasted Victory Memorial at the Village Hall in July 1948 to commemorate those who had fallen in the Second World War. The memorial had originally been erected in 1919 to commemorate those killed in the First World War and the tablet on the front of the memorial was extended to accommodate the additional names.

THE OBJECTS OF THE MOTHERS' UNION.

1. To uphold the Sanctity of Marriage.*

2. To awaken in all Mothers a sense of their great responsibility in the training of their boys and girls — the Fathers and Mothers of the Future.

3. To organise in every place a band of Mothers who will unite in prayer and seek by their own example to lead their families in purity and holiness of life.

* In the words " To uphold the Sanctity of Marriage," the Mothers' Union affirms the Christian principle of the permanence of the relationship between husband and wife.

QUALIFICATIONS OF MEMBERSHIP.

Membership is open to married women :—

1. Who have been baptised, affirm their belief in the principle of infant baptism, and undertake to bring their children (if any) to Holy Baptism.

2. Who accept the teaching contained in the Apostles' Creed.

3. Who are faithful to their marriage vows.

4. Who declare their adherence to the three Central Objects.

Divorce is a disqualification for Membership.

Price 1d.   P. T. O.

THE MOTHERS' UNION
(Incorporated by Royal Charter, 1926).

PREPARATION CARD
for those desiring to become
MEMBERS of the Mothers' Union.

Regulation No. 3. " That there shall be a period of preparation of not less than three months before admission to the Mothers' Union. Any exception to this rule must be sanctioned by the Central President, or by the President of a Federated Council, or by the General President for Ireland. It is intended that preparation should include personal instruction by the Enrolling Member of each prospective Member."

PRAYER.

Prayer is the great bond of union, and you are asked to begin using the following Prayer :—

O LORD, fill us with Thy Holy Spirit, that we may firmly believe in Jesus Christ, and love Him with all our hearts. Wash our souls in His Precious Blood. Make us to hate sin, and to be holy in thought, word and deed. Help us to be faithful wives and loving mothers. Bless us and all who belong to the Mothers' Union, unite us together in love and prayer, and teach us to train our children for Heaven. Pour out Thy Holy Spirit on our husbands and children. Make our homes, Homes of Peace and Love, and may we so live on earth, that we may live with Thee for ever in Heaven ; for Jesus Christ's sake. Amen.

Name *Jean Peake*.

Date and Place of Marriage *16/4/49 St Martin's Brasted*

Date..

Enrolling Member *E.M. Clout*

P. T. O.

Jean Peake's Mothers' Union preparation card, 1949. Note that 'divorce is a disqualification of membership'.

BRASTED ELEEMOSYNARY CHARITIES.

Vacancy for Pension.

The Trustees of these Charities give notice that they will on   the   day of   , 19   proceed to elect a Pensioner to fill a vacancy in the number of Pensioners of the Charities.   The election will take place at   o'clock   on that day at Brasted Rectory.

Poor persons of good character who have been resident in the Parish of Brasted for five years at least, who have not during that period received Poor Law relief, and who from age, ill-health, accident or infirmity, are unable to maintain themselves by their own exertions, are eligible for the appointment.   Preference will be given to those who have shown reasonable providence, and to those who have been longest resident in the Parish.

Application for the appointment must be made in writing to the Trustees, fourteen days at least previously to the election.   Every applicant must state his or her name, address, age and occupation, and must be prepared with sufficient testimonials and other evidence of his or her qualification for the appointment.   Fresh testimonials need not be obtained by any applicant who may have applied when the last vacancy occurred.

Applications should be sent to the Rector.

Hooker Bros., Westerham

Poster advertising a vacancy for a Brasted 'pensioner', about 1950. As well as dispensing annual charitable gifts, Brasted Charities also made regular payments to selected Brasted residents who were especially in need of support.

ORDER No. 2030

Tel. BRASTED 79   Established in 1830

From **F. J. STILL**

Agricultural Engineer :: Coach Builder

THE GREEN, BRASTED, KENT

AGENT for EVERY DESCRIPTION OF AGRICULTURAL MACHINERY

Sept 22nd 19_56_

Miss Dixie Village Hall

Please supply:

1½ Pt _Valspar_	5	3
1 Pt _Valspar_	9	9
1 Pt _Valspar_	9	9
	1 4 9	

Paid 22nd Sept 1959
With Thanks

ORDER/CASH SALE   No. 01837

Brasted Forge Ltd

AGRICULTURAL ENGINEERS · ACETYLENE WELDERS
SHOEING AND GENERAL SMITHS · COACH BUILDERS
DOMESTIC AND HORTICULTURAL SUPPLIES

THE GREEN, BRASTED, KENT

TELEPHONE: BRASTED 656

Mrs Ring   _12 June_ 196_2_

Village Hall

1 Plastic Toilet Seat   13/-

Paid

Telephone 16   Established over 100 Years   **08363**

MARKWICK STORES
(BARCLAY, PERKINS & CO., LTD.)

HIGH-CLASS GROCERS AND PROVISION MERCHANTS

WINES, SPIRITS AND BEERS   HARDWARE AND GARDEN REQUISITES

BRASTED POST OFFICE

9 - 4 - 1954

M Village Hall

2 Bars Fairy Soap.	1	10
Bluebell	1	2
2 Drums Ajax for	1	6
	4	6

Please send receipt to R. C. Husband Mill Meadow Brasted

21874
13 - 5 1954
Received from
M Village Hall
For MARKWICK'S STORES
Sig.   BRASTED.
The sum of £ s. d.
4 6

BRASTED 419   **Brasted,**
       Westerham. Kent.

1966 -

Partners: T. Maudsley
    M. L. Maudsley

_15/12/66_ 196_

M _Brasted Charities_

Dr. to

M. L. MAUDSLEY

Newsagent & Tobacconist

3 Lenbury Fruits 3/3	9	9
lessore	3	3
	6	6

Paid with thanks 15/12/66

Various business receipts from the 1950s and 1960s. M L Maudsley replaced M. Davis in the High Street, M. Davis having produced many of the postcards reproduced in this book, while Brasted Forge is a rare survivor and still going strong.

Further reading

The following selection of books will be useful for anyone wishing to learn more about the long and interesting history of Brasted. The first three books listed are available to view in their entirety online.

Copies of all of these books may be difficult to source due to their age or because they were released with very small print runs. Some of them were published and sold privately making them even more difficult to find. However, copies do turn up from time to time so persistence and vigilance should pay off in the end. The second edition of "Inn of the Few" and the last three books listed are currently in print as at 2020 and should be readily available.

"The History and Topographical Survey of Kent" by Edward Hasted, published by W. Bristow, Canterbury (1797)

"Notes of the Churches in the Counties of Kent, Sussex and Surrey mentioned in the Domesday Book" by the Reverend Arthur Hussey, published by John Russell Smith, London (1852)

"The History of Brasted, its Manor, Parish and Church" by J Cave-Browne, published by J H Jewell, Westerham (1874)

"1496-1946 A Study in Continuity" by C S Durtnell, Brasted, 1946. Re-published by The Caxton and Holmesdale Press (1961)

"Brasted Place and its Owners" by H G H Singleton, Brasted (1954)

"Westerham Valley Railway" by David Gould, published by The Oakwood Press, Trowbridge (1974)

"The School in a Garden" by John Silversides, published by the Trustees of the Tipping Trust for Brasted School (1989)

"A Country Builder, The story of Richard Durtnell and Sons of Brasted 1591-1991" by Hugh Barty-King, published by Henry Melland, London (1991)

"Inn of the Few" by Katherine Preston, published by Spellmount, Tunbridge Wells (1993). Re-ordered and re-published by Valerie Preston (2018)

"The Kentish Scene" by Roland Pym, published by Edwin Taylor, Brasted (2004)

"Brasted Memories" by Karina Jackson, Brasted (2017)

"The Decline and Fall of the Westerham Railway" by Ron Strutt, published by Crecy Publishing (2018)

"St Martin's Church, Brasted, A History and Guide" by Roger Rogowski, published by St Martin's Church, Brasted (2019)

Other books on Kent and South-East England, such as "Kent – The County Books" by Richard Church (1949), "Let's Explore the River Darent" by Frederick G Wood (1983) and "West Kent Within Living

Memory" by the West Kent Federation of Women's Institutes (1995) also contain good references to Brasted and are worth searching out.

Several volumes of 'Bygone Kent', a local history magazine established in 1979, published six times per year, contain interesting articles about various aspects of Brasted's history. Back issues often appear for sale in local second-hand bookshops and online.

Image Credits

This book would not have been possible without the kind and generous support of many people. Grateful thanks are due to the following who kindly provided images for this book.

The images credited to the Brasted Archive were originally compiled by Keith and Celia Smith as part of the Millennium Exhibition displayed in the village hall in 2000.

The images credited to Ben Brooksbank and Lamberhurst are reproduced respectively under Creative Commons Attribution-Sharealike licence 2.0 and Creative Commons Attribution-Sharealike 4.0 International licence.

Every effort has been made to trace the copyright owners of photographs where copyright has not been acknowledged. As far as the publisher has been able to establish, all other photographs are out of copyright and future editions of this book will be amended as and when further information becomes available.

Alderson, Gordon
    Image at top of page(s), 97
Brasted Archive
    Full-page image on page(s), 71, 87, 108, 110
    Image at bottom of page(s), 13, 33, 39, 75, 78, 89, 93, 97, 98, 100
    Image at top of page(s), 30, 46, 85, 89, 90, 98, 99, 100
Brasted Eleemosynary Charities
    Full-page image on page(s), 114
    Image at bottom of page(s), 102
    Image at bottom right of page(s), 115
    Image at top of page(s), 102
Brasted Village Hall Trust
    Full-page image on page(s), 111
    Image at bottom left of page(s), 115
    Images at top of page(s), 115
Brooksbank, Ben
    Image at bottom of page(s), 83
Brown, Ian
    Image at bottom of page(s), 95
Draper, Marc
    Image at top of page(s), 93
George, Frank
    Image at bottom of page(s), 81, 82
    Image at top of page(s), 82
Grosse, Lorna
    Image at bottom of page(s), 38
Jackson, Karina
    Full-page image on page(s), 16, 67, 105
    Image at bottom of page(s), 12, 35, 36, 42, 59, 65, 70, 72, 74, 96

Image at top of page(s), 34, 70, 75, 88
Lamberhurst
    Full-page image on page(s), 80
    Image at top of page(s), 79
Ogley, Bob
    Image at bottom of page(s), 88
Peake, Rob
    Front Cover image
    Full-page image on page(s), 53, 57, 60, 113
    Image at bottom of page(s), 19, 20, 27, 28, 31, 34, 37, 41, 43, 44, 46, 47, 49, 62, 64, 66, 73, 85, 86
    Image at top of page(s), 14, 17, 18, 19, 21, 27, 29, 31, 33, 38, 39, 41, 42, 44, 45, 47, 61, 62, 64, 73, 74, 76, 86
Rich, Elizabeth
    Image at bottom of page(s), 26
    Image at top of page(s), 26, 28
Rogowski, Roger
    Back Cover image
    Full-page image on page(s), 48, 54, 55, 56, 112
    Image at bottom of page(s), 14, 15, 17, 18, 25, 29, 30, 32, 45, 63, 69, 76
    Image at top of page(s), 12, 13, 15, 20, 25, 32, 35, 36, 37, 43, 59, 63, 65, 66, 69, 72, 94
St Martin's Church
    Full-page image on page(s), 50, 51
    Image at bottom of page(s), 99
    Image at top of page(s), 49
Westerham Society/Bill Curtis
    Full-page image on page(s), 104, 106, 107, 109
    Image at bottom of page(s), 21, 22, 23, 61, 79, 90, 91, 94, 103
    Image at top of page(s), 22, 23, 78, 81, 83, 91, 95, 103
Weston, John
    Image at bottom of page(s), 92
    Image at top of page(s), 92, 96

INDEX

4th West Kent Territorials, 90

Air Raid Shelter, 97
Alderson, George, 72, 103
Alma House, 38
Alms Row, 35, 36, 37

Baptist Chapel, 43
Barton family, 41
Bellringing, 99
Black Bull Inn. *See* Public Houses, Bull Inn
Bond's Garage, 33
Bowling Alley, 56
Brasted and Sundridge Football Club, 94
Brasted Carnival, 95
Brasted Cricket Club, 93
Brasted Cross, 71
Brasted Forge, 115
Brasted Hall, 88
Brasted Place, 7, 36, 69, 70, 71, 75, 105
Brasted School, 85, 86
Brasted Village Hall, 34, 106, 112
Bull Cottages, 43
Bull Fields, 60
Burgess, Pharoah, 93

Carriage Works, 21, 22, 23, 93
Chandler & Sons, 104
Church End House, 45, 46, 72, 103
Colinette Cottages, 61
Crawshay, Francis, 49

Darenton, 18, 89
Davis, M. - Newsagent, 28, 29
Day, Arch, 89
Durtnell family, 18, 89
Durtnell, R and Sons, 6, 13
Durtnell, Richard T, 43

Ford's Cottages. *See* Old White Hart
    Cottages
Foxwold, 76, 88

Fuggle's Bakery, 34, 95

Haynes Cottages, 36
Heverswood, 74
Heverswood Lodge, 38
Home Farm, 39
Hop farming, 87

Ivy House, 26

Lambert and Son's, bakery, 32

Markwick's Stores, 25
Maudsley, M L, 115
Mill Farm, 43, 44, 89
Mill House, 34, 95
Mothers' Union, 99, 113

National School. *See* Brasted School

Old Forge Cottages, 30, 96
Old Rectory, The, 5, 6, 72
Old White Hart Cottages, 12, 27

Philippines, 73
Preston, Kathy, 15
Preston, Teddy (Edward), 15, 98
Public Houses
    Bull Inn, 37, 38, 60, 103
    Fox and Hounds, 6
    King's Arms, 32
    Stanhope Arms, 6, 45, 46
    Star Inn, 61
    Tally Ho, The, 63
    White Hart, 13, 14
Puddledock Lane, 64
Pym Family, 76, 88

Queen's Arms. *See* Public Houses,
    Stanhope Arms

Scords Lane, 66

Stanhope, James 1st Earl, 45
Stanhope, James 7th Earl, 98
Stanhope, Philip, 1st Baron Weardale, 73
Stocket Chapel, 110
Streatfield House, 29
Swimming Bath, 90, 91, 106, 108

Tannery Cottages, 57
The Manse, 43
Tilings, 30, 31, 32, 96
Tipping Estate, 30, 36, 39, 72, 103
Tipping, William, 7, 34, 36, 69
Tipping, William Fearon, 70, 105
Tolstoy, Countess Alexandra, 73
Toys Hill village hall, 64, 65

Toys Hill well, 64, 65
Turton, John, 7, 69, 71

Vines Gate, 75

War Memorial, 35, 110, 112
Waterhouse. Alfred, 48
Watts, Lewis - Butcher, 29, 100
Weardale Manor, 73
Wells, Annie, 38
West Kent Foxhounds, 14, 21
Withers' Stores, 32
Woodhams & Sons, 26, 28
World War One, 35, 41, 94
World War Two, 16